IN THE
MASTER'S STEPS

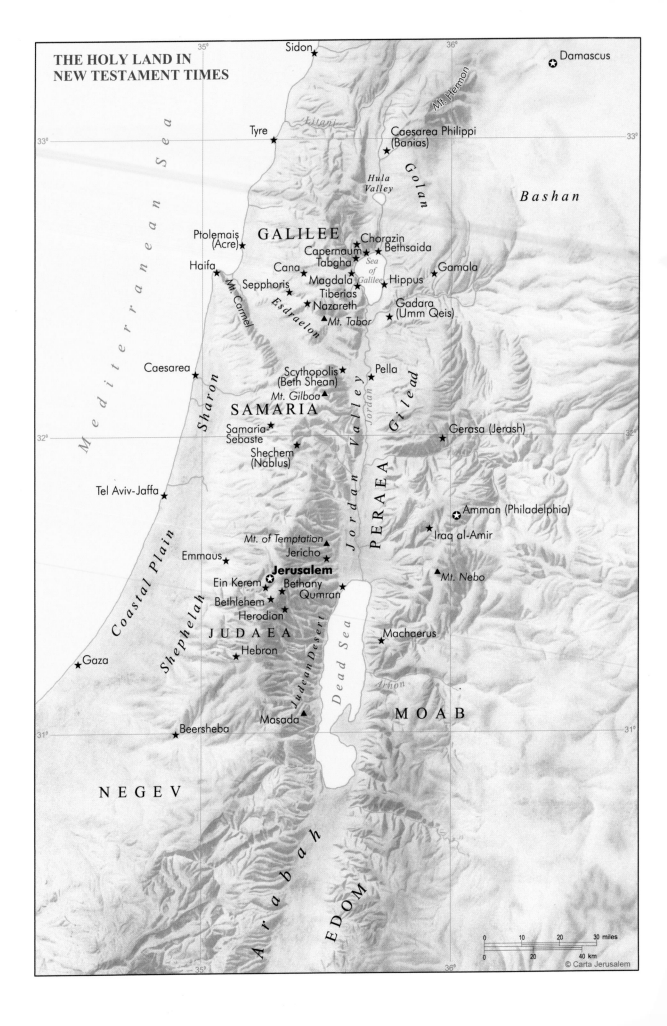

THE HOLY LAND IN NEW TESTAMENT TIMES

Sidon

Damascus

Mt. Hermon

Litani

Tyre

Caesarea Philippi (Banias)

Hula Valley

Golan

Bashan

Ptolemais (Acre)

GALILEE

Chorazin

Capernaum

Bethsaida

Haifa

Cana

Tabgha

Sea of Galilee

Gamala

Mt. Carmel

Sepphoris

Magdala

Hippus

Tiberias

Gadara (Umm Qeis)

Esdraelon

Nazareth

▲*Mt. Tabor*

Mediterranean Sea

Caesarea

Scythopolis (Beth Shean)

Pella

Mt. Gilboa ▲

Sharon

SAMARIA

Gilead

Samaria Sebaste

Gerasa (Jerash)

Jordan

Shechem (Nablus)

Jordan Valley

Tel Aviv-Jaffa

PERAEA

Amman (Philadelphia)

Mt. of Temptation ▲

Iraq al-Amir

Emmaus

Jericho

Coastal Plain

Ein Kerem

Jerusalem

▲ *Mt. Nebo*

Bethany

Bethlehem

Qumran

Herodion

Shephelah

JUDAEA

Hebron

Judean Desert

Dead Sea

Machaerus

Gaza

Arnon

M O A B

Masada ▲

Beersheba

N E G E V

Arabah

E D O M

| 0 | | 10 | 20 | 30 miles |

| 0 | 20 | 40 km |

VOLUME ONE

IN THE MASTER'S STEPS
THE GOSPELS IN THE LAND

R. STEVEN NOTLEY

cartaJerusalem

First published in 2014 by
CARTA Jerusalem

Partially excerpted from
The Sacred Bridge: Carta's Atlas of the Biblical World
Carta Jerusalem 2014

Cartography: Carta Jerusalem
Cover photograph: Shmuel Magal
   The Plain of Gennesaret and the Sea of Galilee, as viewed from Mount Arbel

Great care has been taken to cite all sources of illustrations whenever known. If inadvertently we failed to
do so, due credit will be given in the following edition.

ISBN: 978-965-220-851-4

Printed in Israel

CONTENTS

Preface.. 6

CHAPTER 1

The Birth of Jesus and the Flight into Egypt.. 9

  The Division of Herod's Kingdom, 4 B.C.–A.D. 6 10

  The Return from Egypt; The Boy Jesus in the Temple 13

CHAPTER 2

The Ministry of John and the Baptism of Jesus 15

  The Baptism of Jesus and the Sojourn in the Wilderness

CHAPTER 3

The Travels of Jesus.. 21

  From Nazareth to Cana and Capernaum

CHAPTER 4

The Sea of Galilee: Development of an Early Christian Toponym 25

  Jesus' Travels in the Districts of Tyre and Caesarea Philippi 28

  The "Way to the Sea" According to Isaiah...29

CHAPTER 5

The First Century Environs of the Sea of Galilee 31

  Around the Sea of Galilee...33

  The Plain of Bethsaida..43

  The Cities of the Decapolis...52

CHAPTER 6

The Last Days of Jesus.. 55

  Jesus' Last Journey to Jerusalem 56

  Jericho Area Today 57

  Plan of Roman Jericho..57

CHAPTER 7

Jesus and the Myth of an Essene Quarter in Jerusalem 61

  Plan of Qumran...63

  Jerusalem at the Time of Jesus 68

CHAPTER 8

The Arrest and Death of Jesus 69

  Caesarea—Plan of the City...72

  The Arrest, Interrogation and Execution of Jesus 74

CHAPTER 9

From the Empty Tomb to the Road to Emmaus 77

  The Resurrection and Ascension 80

Index.. 83

PREFACE

The Evangelists who penned our four Gospels wrote at different historical points and each with a distinctive theological perspective. Yet, the geographical underpinning of their narratives—for the most part—has escaped these variations. Indeed, they wrote under the assumption that their readers possessed an intimate familiarity with the topographical setting for the story. Unfortunately, for the vast majority of Christian readers of the New Testament this is not the case.

Our Gospels are not unique in this regard. A parallel may be drawn to the writings of the first-century Jewish historian, Flavius Josephus. A generation ago scholars put little trust in the reliability of his report. It is true that he wrote mostly from the comfort of his perch overlooking the Tiber River in Rome, having taken on the surname of the Roman emperors, Vespasian and Titus; and there is little question that his indebtedness to his imperial benefactors colored his account of recent events, which had erupted in the Jewish rebellion against Rome in A.D. 66–73.

Nevertheless, Josephus was born and raised in Roman Judaea. He walked the streets of Jerusalem and had been entrusted with building the Jewish defenses of the Galilee. So, his first-hand knowledge of both the physical setting of Herodian Jerusalem and the geographical region of Galilee was extensive. Archaeology over the last fifty years has confirmed his description of many of the physical realities of Judean topography and the Herodian building projects completed in the decades before the revolt. As a consequence, there has evolved an increasing esteem for the writings of Josephus and—when read critically—their witness to the tumultuous events that ended in the destruction of Jerusalem and its Temple.

A similar re-appreciation among scholars has emerged regarding the geographical, historical and even the religious details imbedded in the narratives of our canonical Gospels. A generation ago, the German theologian Hans Conzelmann could write comfortably from Tübingen—having never stepped foot in the land of Israel—about Luke's "geographical ineptitude" and suggest that concerning the Sea of Galilee in the Third Gospel, "the lake is more of a theological than geographical factor." In fact, the realities of Galilean topography and specifically those of the Sea of Galilee indicate just the opposite. One wonders how Conzelmann was able to reconcile the

Evangelist's alleged geographical ineptitude with the fact that Luke alone of the Gospel writers consistently and correctly describes the Sea of Galilee as a freshwater lake (Greek: *limne*) and not brackish seawater (Greek: *thalassa*). Such concern for details is hardly the penchant of a writer who ineptly jettisoned geography for theology.

Further, recent archaeological efforts at New Testament sites have added to our understanding of historical geography and demonstrated that in many cases the Gospels present our most ancient and reliable witness to the physical stage onto which Jesus stepped. This is not to suggest a naïve, simplistic reading of the Gospels. Modern scientific advances—e.g., linguistic, literary, historical, and socioreligious approaches—are still essential, if we are to read these ancient stories seriously.

Yet, the new information has brought renewed attention to the importance of the land in our reading of the Gospels. This is not a modern novelty, however, but a re-discovery of the important role geography has in our reading of these well-known passages. Such an eye to topography was already embraced by the fifth-century monk, who translated the Bible in the shadow of the Church of Nativity in Bethlehem.

> Five gospels record the life of Jesus. Four you will find in books and the one you will find in the land they call Holy. Read the fifth gospel and the world of the four will open to you. St. Jerome (A.D. 347–420)

There is both an art and a science in reading ancient history through a geographical lens. On the following pages we have brought recent advances in history, geography, toponomy, and archaeology, the tools necessary to shed fresh light on the Gospels. The hope is that a better understanding of the physical setting and events that framed the life of Jesus can assist us to hear more clearly the message he proclaimed.

R. S. Notley
July 2014

Main entrance to the Church of the Nativity in Bethlehem. (photo Mike Horton)

CHAPTER 1

THE BIRTH OF JESUS AND THE FLIGHT INTO EGYPT

ARK AND JOHN OPEN THEIR GOSPELS with the ministry of John the Baptist, while Matthew and Luke provide details of Jesus' birth. Even though the two birth narratives give different historical perspectives, they both identify the place of Jesus' birth at Bethlehem (Matt 2:1; Luke 2:15)—the ancestral home of King David (1 Sam 17:12). The relationship between Jesus and David is a particular emphasis of Matthew: "An account of the genealogy of Jesus the Messiah, *the son of David*, the son of Abraham" (Matt 1:1; 12:23 *et passim*).

By contrast, John's Gospel lacks both the title "son of David" and any mention of a Bethlehem birth. When the subject of Jesus' birthplace is raised, the Evangelist leaves unanswered the objection of some:

> Still others asked, "How can the Christ come from Galilee? Does not the Scripture say that the Christ will come from David's family and from Bethlehem, the town where David lived?" (John 7:41–42)

Luke records that Joseph and Mary were residents of Nazareth in Galilee (Luke 1:26, 2:4), and that they traveled to Bethlehem in compliance with a census ordered by Caesar Augustus when Quirinius was governor of Syria (Luke 2:2). Joseph's enrollment at Bethlehem suggests that he originated from the Judean region south of Jerusalem. Luke does not explain what brought Joseph to Nazareth in the years before Jesus was born.

We also possess scant information outside of the New Testament about this Galilean village (see Eus. *Onom.* 138:14; Epiph. *Adv. haer.* 30.11.10). Josephus makes no mention of Nazareth, and rabbinic tradition reports only that it was a village of priests (*Mishmarot* 18; *Qoh. Rab.* 2:8). The scarcity of its mention is not surprising. Modern archaeological work in Nazareth paints a picture of a remote, insignificant village that would have attracted little attention.

Both Matthew and Luke present Jesus' birth during the last years of Herod the Great, who died in 4 B.C. (Matt 2:1; Luke 1:5). New Testament scholarship has tried to reconcile Herod's presence in the birth narratives with Luke's report that Jesus was born at the same time as the Roman census when Quirinius was governor (Luke 2:2). Luke and Josephus are familiar with another census that took place in A.D. 6 (Acts 5:37; *J.W.* 7:253), but there is no mention in Jewish or Roman sources of an earlier census under Quirinius during the reign of Herod the Great.

External corroboration is also lacking for Matthew's account of Herod's execution of the young male children in Bethlehem. Matthew is our only record of the event. Nevertheless, Herod's actions described by Matthew fit the king's paranoid personality sketched by Josephus. Herod executed members of his own family out of fear that they might attempt to usurp the throne. On one occasion, certain Pharisees prophesied to the wife of Pheroras—the brother of Herod—that, "by God's decree Herod's throne would be taken from him, both from himself and his descendants, and the royal power would fall to her and Pheroras and to any children that they might have…" (*Ant.* 17:41–45). Herod responded by killing the Pharisees involved and the members of his family who had expressed sympathy with this prophecy.

THE DIVISION OF HEROD'S KINGDOM, 4 B.C.–A.D. 6

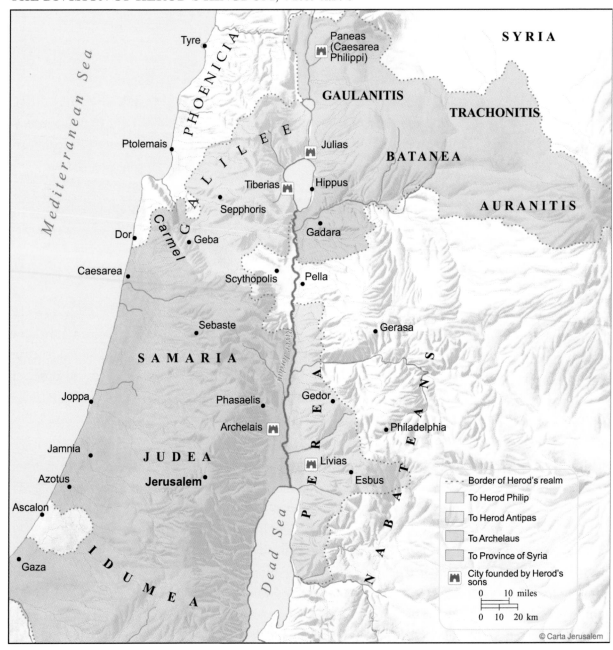

(above) Herodium: view of the mountain palace-fortress from Lower Herodium, likely the site of Herod's burial. (photo S. Magal)

(left) Coin (reverse side) of Herod Archelaus (4 B.C.–A.D. 6) showing a war-galley with oars and cabin at stern.

Matthew 2:13–15 reports that Joseph was warned by an angel to take his family to Egypt to escape Herod's murderous intentions. Only when the king had died was it safe to return to the Land of Israel. In the meantime, Rome had awarded authority in the region of Judea and Samaria to Archelaus, son of Herod (*J.W.* 2:93; *Ant.* 17:317). He followed in his father's cruel footsteps. So, according to Matthew, Joseph was warned in a dream not to return to the environs of Jerusalem.

And he [Joseph] went and dwelt in a city called Nazareth, that what was spoken by the prophets might be fulfilled, "He [Jesus] will be called a Nazarene." (RSV Matt 2:23)

This final verse of Matthew's report concerning Jesus' birth and childhood has challenged Christian readers for centuries. The crux of its interpretation revolves around the meaning of *Nazoraios* that is routinely translated Nazarene, and the identification of the prophecy that Matthew claims is fulfilled with the family's settlement in Nazareth.

We will not review the many and varied solutions that have been proposed. We venture here only two observations about the language of the verse that may assist towards narrowing Matthew's possible intent. First, the "o" in the second syllable of *Nazoraios* indicates that the Hebrew

The flight into Egypt (Matt 2:14), *engraving from a 19th century Bible.* (Carta collection)

word behind our Greek term was *natzor*, i.e., one kept, protected, and not *netzer* (branch) or *nazir* (Nazirite). Second, translators of our verse rarely take note that the passive Greek verb can be intended to communicate a divine passive in which God is assumed to be acting. The verse may thus be rendered, "The one whom I have kept (i.e., *natzori*) shall be called (i.e., by God)." Accordingly, Matthew's elliptical allusion is to a prophetic passage that describes one who has been kept, protected and whom the Lord has called.

Scholarship on this verse has focused most of its attention on trying to explain the significance of the collocation of the Greek words *Nazoraios* and *Nazaret*. Yet, nowhere else in the New Testament do these terms appear alongside each other. Could it be that Matthew has brought the elliptical

משמרת ראשונה יהויריב מסרביי מרון
משמרת שניה ידעיה עמוק צפורים
משמרת שלישית חרים מפשטה
משמרת רביעית שערים עיתהלו
משמרת חמישית מלכיה בית לחם
משמרת ששית מיין יודפת
משמרת שביעית הקוץ עילבו
משמרת שמינית אביה כפר עוזיה
משמרת תשיעית ישוע ארבל
משמרת עשירית שכניה חבודת כבול
משמרת אחת עשרה אלישיב כהן קנה
משמרת שתים עשרה יקים פשחור צפת
משמרת שלוש עשרה חופה בית מעון
משמרת ארבע עשרה ישבאב בית עצית שיחין
משמרת חמש עשרה בלגה מעריה בלגה זיונית
משמרת שש עשרה אימר פרן מרה
משמרת שבע עשרה חזיר ממליח
משמרת שמונה עשרה הפיצץ נצרת
משמרת תשע עשרה פתחיה כול עב
משמרת עשרים יחזקאל בעזרלנא
משמרת אחת ועשרים יכין כפר יוחנה
משמרת שתים ועשרים גמול בית חוביה
משמרת שלוש ועשרים דליה הגתון צלמין
משמרת ארבע ועשרים מעזיה חמת אריח

Reconstruction of a Byzantine Hebrew inscription, found in excavations at Caesarea in 1962, with a list of priestly courses in which a family from Nazareth is mentioned. According to Mishmarot *18 a priestly family settled in Nazareth, and likewise* Midrash Qohelet *2:8 attests to the priestly character of Nazareth (shaded sections indicate the fragments that were found).*

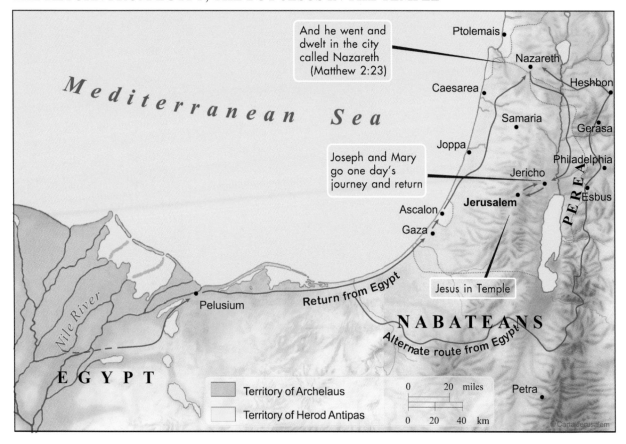

Old Testament prophecy, not because of the name of the Galilean village, but because the angelic warning and protective actions of Joseph were reminiscent of an ancient prophecy?

A cruel son of Herod remained in power in Jerusalem, and it was not yet safe to return there. At the angelic warning, Joseph took Mary and Jesus to Nazareth out of concern for their continued safety. Their relocation to the security of this remote Galilean village, where Jesus could grow to adulthood, reminded Matthew of a verse concerning the Isaianic Servant of the Lord:

> *I, the Lord, have called you* in righteousness; I will take hold of your hand. *I will keep you* and will make you to
> be a covenant for the people and a light for the nations. (Isa 42:6)

So, Matthew concludes his abbreviated description of Jesus' infancy with a report that Jesus was taken to a remote village in Galilee and preserved there by the Lord, until the appointed time for the beginning of his prophetic ministry. We witness a similar literary device by Luke to summarize and conclude his report concerning the childhood of John the Baptist: "And the child grew and became strong in spirit; and he lived in the desert until he appeared publicly to Israel" (Luke 1:80).

Of additional value for Matthew, however, the Evangelist uses Isaiah 42:6 to anticipate the next episode in his record of Jesus' life—the heavenly call at his baptism (Matt 3:16–17). Scholars have already demonstrated that according to the Evangelists the heavenly voice drew from the same block of scripture in Isaiah 42 to proclaim the prophetic significance of Jesus' baptism: "Here is my servant, whom I uphold, my chosen one in whom I delight; I will put my Spirit on him" (Isa 42:1).

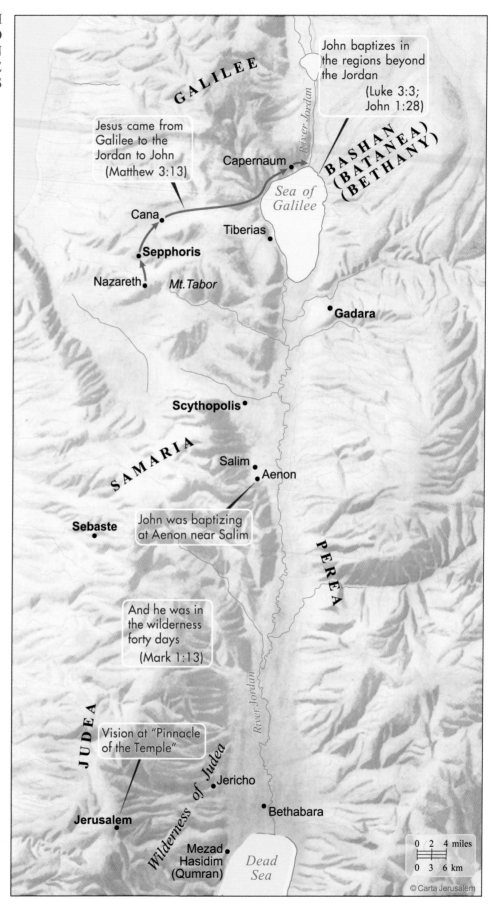

John baptizes in
the regions beyond
the Jordan
(Luke 3:3;
John 1:28)

GALILEE

River Jordan

Jesus came from
Galilee to the
Jordan to John
(Matthew 3:13)

Capernaum

*BASHAN
(BATANEA)
(BETHANY)*

Cana

*Sea of
Galilee*

Tiberias

Sepphoris

Nazareth

Mt. Tabor

Gadara

Scythopolis

SAMARIA

Salim

Aenon

Sebaste

John was baptizing
at Aenon near Salim

PEREA

And he was in
the wilderness
forty days
(Mark 1:13)

JUDEA

Vision at "Pinnacle
of the Temple"

River Jordan

Wilderness of Judea

Jericho

Jerusalem

Bethabara

Mezad
Hasidim
(Qumran)

*Dead
Sea*

0 2 4 miles

0 3 6 km

© Carta Jerusalem

CHAPTER 2

THE MINISTRY OF JOHN AND THE BAPTISM OF JESUS

EOGRAPHICAL SETTING. In all of the Gospels the ministry of Jesus begins with his participation in the baptism of John. The geographical setting for John's ministry varies in the four Gospel accounts. In both Christian tradition and modern scholarship this has resulted in uncertainty regarding the location of John. All of the accounts cite Isaiah 40:3 to introduce the reason for the Baptist's presence in the wilderness. "A voice cries: In the wilderness prepare the way of the Lord." Like the Qumran Congregation (1QS 8:13–14), John believed that preparation for the Lord should take place in the wilderness.

Mark reports that John was "in the wilderness" (Mark 1:4) without any specification where that wilderness lay. The Greek term, similar to its Hebrew counterpart, need not indicate an arid, uninhabitable place, i.e., desert. It may also describe unpopulated, pasturing areas belonging to residents of a nearby city (cf. Luke 8:29). So, we hear of a "wilderness" near Bethsaida (Luke 9:10–12), where Mark describes green grass (Mark 6:39). We find a similar breadth of usage for the Hebrew term in the Old Testament (Gen 21:14; Joel 2:22; Isa 42:11).

Mark does record that crowds came to John from "all Judea and Jerusalem" (Mark 1:5; cf. Matt 3:5; John 1:19), which may or may not imply proximity to the arid regions in the lower Jordan Valley. It is difficult to know how much weight Mark intends for us to give to these geographical details about the crowds. Are they instead the Evangelist's periphrastic style of emphasizing John's role as the Voice of Isaiah 40:3? In the Isaiah passage the Voice is to speak to Jerusalem and the cities of Judea (Isa 40:9).

If Mark is employing here a technique of verbal allusion, it would not be the only instance. For example, elsewhere he omits explicit testimony to the popular notion that the Baptist was Elijah redivivus (cf. Mal 4:5 [HMT 3:23]; Matt 11:14; Luke 1:17). Yet, Mark was certainly aware of this opinion, because he describes John's clothing with clear intent to present John in Elijah's attire (Mark 1:6; Matt 3:4; 2 Kgs 1:8). On that occasion, Markan detail is not intended to merely describe John's clothing but to signal to his readers the eschatological importance of John's prophetic role. The challenge for the modern reader remains how to read these Markan details. Matthew on both of these occasions shares Mark's features, but he alone of the Synoptic Gospels—perhaps anticipating the mention of the Jerusalem and Judean crowds or reflecting the earlier Judean wilderness setting of Isaiah 40:3—specifies that John was in "the wilderness of Judea" (Matt 3:1).

While Luke agrees with Mark's portrayal that John is in the wilderness, he lacks Mark and Matthew's geographical reference to Judean and Jerusalem crowds. Instead, Luke notes only, "[John] went into all the region about the Jordan" (Luke 3:3). The Fourth Gospel contributes unique geographical details about the location of John's ministry, before and after its description of John's baptism of Jesus. At points the Evangelist parallels the Synoptic Gospels, and at other points he presents independent traditions. Of the setting prior to Jesus' baptism, John's Gospel records that the Baptist was at "Bethany beyond the Jordan" (John 1:28). Sometime later he is reported at "Aenon near Salim" (John 3:23). So, in apparent agreement, John and Luke present the Baptist moving between different venues and not limited to any single location.

The site of Bethany in the Transjordan finds no mention in early literature outside of John's singular reference. Origen reports in c. A.D. 200 that no such place exists (Orig. Comm. John VI.24). In spite of his admission that "[Bethany] is found in almost all of the copies [of John's Gospel]," he proposed a textual emendation for the verse to read Bethabara. Eusebius' *Onomasticon* (58:18) a century later describes Bethabara: "Where John was baptizing, beyond the Jordan. The place

The baptism of Jesus as depicted in the Church of St. John the Baptist, Ein Kerem. (photo S. Magal)

The wilderness of Judea. (photo S. Magal)

is shown where even today many of the brothers still endeavor to receive a bath." Eusebius embraced this textual solution first heard from Origen, because he makes no mention of Bethany in connection with John's baptism. While these early Christian conjectures exchanged the known for the unknown, manuscript support for Bethabara prior to Origen is nonexistent. Bethany appears in our earliest and best manuscripts of John's Gospel. Confusion in the later Byzantine period is compounded by the Medeba Map, which preserves "Bethabara, the sanctuary of Saint John the Baptist" on the *western* bank of the Jordan River, not as the New Testament describes Bethany, "beyond (i.e., *east of*) the Jordan."

John's reference to Aenon shares Bethany's absence in the early sources. The Medeba Map describes an Aenon in the Transjordan and identifies it with the site of Sapsaphas. A second "Aenon near Salim" is depicted on the west side of the Jordan River not too distant from Scythopolis (i.e., Beth-shean). This latter site is attested also in Eusebius' *Onomasticon* 40:1–4 and Egeria's *Travels* 15:1–4. A third suggestion for Aenon, perhaps owing to the fact that mention of Aenon occurs within the Fourth Gospel's narrative about Jesus in Samaria, identifies the Baptist in the interior of the hill country of Samaria. Its location is remembered near the modern-day Arab village of Salim (Jdt 4:4). While the toponymic challenge of springs (=Aenon) near Salim may be resolved, it is difficult to understand how the interior of Samaria served as the venue for John's ministry to call Jews to repentance and ritual immersion. Identification of an early Roman location for the springs of Aenon remains uncertain.

Returning to Bethany, it is suggested that the reference in John 1:28 is not to a village, but to the region of Bashan in the Transjordan. Designation of the region of biblical Bashan—extending from Mount Hermon in the north to the southern boundaries of the Lower Golan—with the term Batanea is also heard by Greek writers from Josephus (*Life* 54; *Ant.* 9:159) to Eusebius (*Onom.* 44:9–11). Additionally, according to the Septuagint the region of Bashan is demarked like Bethany, "beyond the Jordan" (Deut 4:47; Josh 9:10).

If "Bethany beyond the Jordan" does signal the region of ancient Bashan (Batanea), then it indicates that John's ministry reached regions northeast of the Sea of Galilee. A northern setting for John better suits the description that two of his disciples, Andrew and Peter, together with Philip came out from Bethsaida to follow Jesus the day following his baptism (John 1:44). The location of John's disciples at Bethsaida on the northern shores of the Sea of Galilee is not easily reconciled with the traditional location of Jesus' baptism in the lower Jordan Valley near Jericho.

It may be of some significance that in rabbinic opinion, the waters of the Jordan River above the Sea of Galilee were preferable for ritual immersion. The waters of the Yarmuk and lower Jordan rivers were reckoned unsuitable, since they included "mixed waters" (*m. Parah* 8:10).

In other words, these rivers south of the Sea of Galilee received tributaries of questionable purity. The rabbinic estimation accords with the lack of any mention of the practice of Jewish ritual immersion in the lower Jordan River in the days of the Second Temple.

John's ministry in the north seems a more fitting setting for his critique of actions involving the Herodian families, who resided in Galilee and the north. John's popularity and outspoken critique resulted in his imprisonment by Herod Antipas, tetrarch of Galilee. Josephus mistakenly transcribes the mention of Macherus from a few lines earlier and repeats it to identify the place where John was imprisoned and executed (*Ant.* 18:119). Such a location for these events is highly unlikely and probably indicates the historian did not know where John died. In addition, Mark's description that "leading officials of Galilee" (Mark 6:21) were present during the banquet when John was condemned, strengthens the contention that John was imprisoned and executed in Antipas' Galilean palace in Tiberias.

John's calling to the crowds to repent and ritually immerse in the regions of the Jordan above the Sea of Galilee may also explain the large crowds (*Ant.* 18:118) that Jesus encountered on the plains near

John the Baptist
(Hagia Sophia, Istanbul; photo R. S. Notley)

Qasr el-Yahud, south of the Sea of Galilee, is thought by some to be the traditional site of the Baptism. (photo S. Magal)

Bethsaida, where he withdrew upon hearing of the Baptist's death (Matt 14:13). According to Mark, when Jesus saw the crowds he had compassion for them, "because they were like sheep without a shepherd" (Mark 6:34). With these words the Evangelist hints both to the relationship of the crowds with the recently deceased John, and the popular notion among some that John was the anticipated prophet-like Moses (Deut 18:18; John 1:25; cf. 4Q175 1:5–8). Mark's creative use of the phrase—"sheep without a shepherd"—is intended to echo the same words spoken by the Lord to Moses in Numbers 27:17 to emphasize the need for new leadership after his death.

What we witness, then, with the topographical setting for the Feeding of the Multitudes in the Synoptic Gospels (Luke 9:10–17 *parr.*) is not unlike the Fourth Gospel's fragmented description of Jesus' return beyond the Jordan.

> Then Jesus returned beyond the Jordan to the place where John had been baptizing in the early days (i.e., Batanea/Bashan; John 1:28). Here he stayed and many people came to him. They said, "Though John never performed a miraculous sign, all that John said about this man was true." And in that place many believed in Jesus.
>
> (John 10:40–42)

FROM NAZARETH TO CANA AND CAPERNAUM

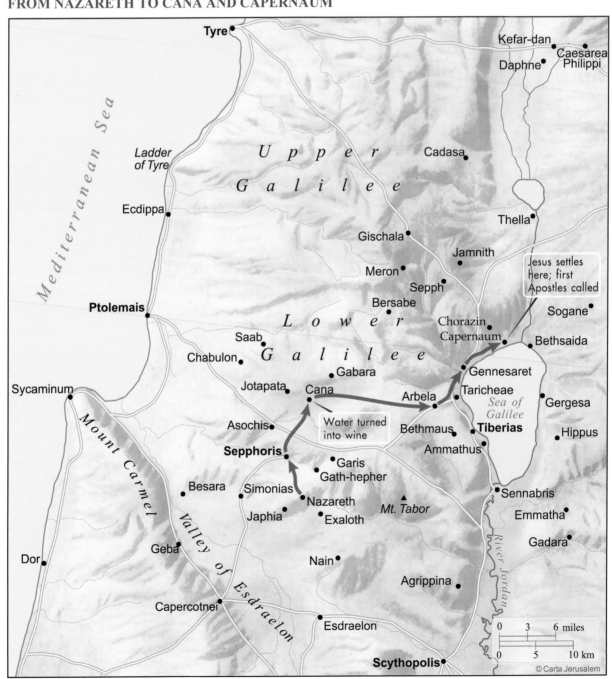

CHAPTER 3

THE TRAVELS
OF JESUS

ᖴROM NAZARETH TO CAPERNAUM. Prominent east-west valleys (Beth-haccerem, Hannathon, Bêt Netôfa, Turân) that traverse the lower region are one of the topographical features that distinguishes Lower Galilee from Upper Galilee (*J.W.* 3:35). The valleys of Lower Galilee are the result of prehistoric tectonic activity. These geological striations extend from the Mediterranean coast north of Mount Carmel and reach inland to the Sea of Galilee and the upper Jordan Valley.

By contrast the Upper Galilee region lacks the open valley systems that mark Lower Galilee, and so was not easily traversed. In addition, its mountainous terrain reaches heights that double those of the mountains of Lower Galilee. The contrasting degree of accessibility left its mark on human settlement and movement in both regions. Archaeological surveys in Lower Galilee indicate a greater degree of outside contact that is evidenced in the material culture of the populations residing there. Moreover, while Josephus attests to the establishment of new urban centers (Sepphoris, Tiberias, Gabara: *Life* 123) in Lower Galilee during the Hellenistic and early Roman periods, there is no similar evidence for urban centers in Upper Galilee.

The topographical delineation between Upper and Lower Galilee is the esh-Shaghûr fault that is marked by the Beth-haccerem Valley, the northernmost of the transversal valleys in Lower Galilee. The accessibility of the Lower Galilee region caused by these valleys had its impact on social development. There was sparse settlement in the interior of Upper Galilee, while the early capital of Galilee was Sepphoris, positioned in the Bêt Netôfa Valley (Sahl el-Battôf). Its importance was accentuated by its location at the crossroads of the Ptolemais–Taricheae (Magdala) trunk road and the secondary north-south route by way of Simonias to the Jezreel Valley and the international coastal highway.

In Matthew 4:13 the Evangelist reports that Jesus traveled from Nazareth to Capernaum. The journey north from Nazareth and east may pass through either the Bêt Netôfa Valley or the Turân Basin to descend from Nazareth's chalk ridge overlooking the Jezreel Valley to villages along the Sea of Galilee. However, indications of Jesus' presence in the Bêt Netôfa Valley suggest that he used the Ptolemais–Taricheae trunk road in his movement between his boyhood home and the Sea of Galilee.

In the beginnings of the Fourth Gospel Jesus' first miracle is recorded at Cana (John 2:1–11). Immediately following the miracle Jesus is reported to descend to Capernaum (John 2:12). According to John, on another occasion Cana and Capernaum are likewise juxtaposed in mention of Jesus' activity (John 4:46). It should also be remembered that Cana was the home of one of Jesus' twelve disciples, Nathana-el (John 1:45–49, 21:2). Together these verses suggest Jesus' presence in Cana on more than one occasion and that the village may have been a regular waystation on his route from Nazareth to the Sea of Galilee.

The New Testament site for Cana of Galilee is likely Khirbet Qanah in the Bêt Netôfa Valley. It guarded the ascent to Jotapata, the city of Josephus, who reports staying in Cana (*Life* 86). The fortified village lay on the road from Ptolemais to Taricheae (Magdala). The Hellenistic-Roman site is currently under excavation and should be distinguished from the medieval Christian pilgrimage site of Kafr Kana that from the time of Quaresmius (A.D. 1620) has been identified as New Testament Cana.

Eusebius (Eus. *Onom.* 116:4) identifies the New Testament village with the Old Testament Kanah of Joshua 19:28. However, this is merely a result of the similarity of the Septuagint's Greek rendering of the Hebrew name for the Old Testament village rather than a clear identification. The lack of any topographical information by Eusebius other than his biblical citation is patent for sites unknown to him. His knowledge of Galilee was limited in any event. However, it seems that by the late Roman period the identity of either Old Testament Kanah or New Testament Cana was unknown.

The journey from Nazareth to Capernaum is almost 30 miles (48 km), too lengthy for a single day's travel. Instead, Cana provided a convenient break in the journey, lying as it did on the

The Christian pilgrimage site of Cana (Kafr Kana) in Galilee. (photo S. Magal)

View of the Arbel Pass in Galilee. (photo S. Magal)

Ptolemais–Taricheae (Magdala) road. Accessibility to the Sea of Galilee from Cana is indicated by Josephus' report of an overnight march from Cana to Tiberias in the company of two hundred men (*Life* 86–90). His report demonstrates that the route from Cana to the Sea of Galilee was known and in use. Finally, the Johannine account of the nobleman's appeal for Jesus to heal his son (John 4:46–54) assumes his travel from Capernaum to Cana, where Jesus was staying. While questions may exist concerning certain geographical details in the event, especially in terms of its relationship to its Synoptic counterpart, clearly the author of the Fourth Gospel saw no problem in describing a journey from Cana to Capernaum.

Khirbet Qanah lies a little more than 7 miles (11 km) north of Nazareth. Several ridge routes lead down the northern slopes of the Nazareth ridge into the Bêt Netôfa Valley. Travel to Cana likely led near to Sepphoris that lies in the middle of the valley. The route from Cana to Capernaum then courses north and east along the northern edges of the Bêt Netôfa Valley until it descends into Wâdī Arbel. This serpentine descent winds north of Qarné Hittim through the Arbel Pass. Passing at the foot of the Arbel cliffs the route turns north across the fertile Plain of Gennesaret and follows the shoreline past Magdala to Capernaum.

The Sea of Galilee at sunset. (photo S. Ben-Yosef)

CHAPTER 4

THE SEA OF GALILEE: DEVELOPMENT OF AN EARLY CHRISTIAN TOPONYM

NEW TESTAMENT SCHOLARSHIP has long recognized that there are toponyms that find no mention outside of the New Testament. Prominent among those are two sites that appear in the Passion narratives of Jesus: Gethsemane (Matt 26:36; Mark 14:32) and Golgotha (Matt 27:33; Mark 15:22; John 19:17). These terms draw immediate notice, because they appear to transliterate Semitic toponyms. Less attention has been given to another place name of equal rarity: the Sea of Galilee (Matt 4:18, 15:29; Mark 1:16, 3:7, 7:31; John 6:1).

The uncommon nature of this place name is indicated in the Fourth Gospel by the Evangelist's need to further define it with an additional name more familiar to his readers: "After this Jesus went to the other side of the Sea of Galilee [which is the Sea] *of Tiberias*" (John 6:1). The city of Tiberias, built by Herod Antipas on the lakeshore (*Ant.* 18:36; *J.W.* 2:168), appears again at the end of the Gospel to identify the lake (John 21:1: the Sea of Tiberias) without the previous geographical marker "of Galilee". The Johannine toponym parallels both Josephus (*J.W.* 3:57) and the classical authors, Pausanias (*Descr.* 5.7.4) and Solinus (*Collectanea Rerum Memorabilium* 35:3: "Sara is a lake that extends sixteen miles…it is the Lake of Tiberias").

The fourth-century writer, Julius Honorius, likewise employed the city of Tiberias (*Cosmographia* 2: *the sea of Tiberias*), but he alone among the Latin authors uses the term *mare* (i.e., sea) rather than *lacus* (i.e., lake) to describe the lake. There is some question whether Julius was a pagan or a Christian. Julius' rare combination of *sea* with *Tiberias* that only occurs elsewhere in the Fourth Gospel suggests that the Roman author may have at least been familiar with the Christian work.

The most numerous and detailed references to the lake are those by Josephus. He consistently calls the body of water a lake rather than a sea. His personal familiarity with the body of water likely led to his practice of referring to it simply as "the lake", without any additional topographical determinant (*Life* 96, 153, 165, 304, 327; *J.W.* 2:635). As previously noted, on two occasions he identifies the lake with Tiberias (*J.W.* 3:57, 4:456). More often, however, he uses the toponym used by the inhabitants of the region: "…the lake, which the native inhabitants call Gennesar" (*J.W.* 3:463; see also 2:573; 3:506; *Ant.* 18:28, 36). The commonplace identification of the lake with Gennesar is further indicated by references to the body of water simply as "the Gennesar" (*J.W.* 3:515, 516; cf. *Ant.* 5:84).

The passage cited above by Solinus identified the lake with Tiberias, as well as a place called *Sara*. This is certainly a reference to Gennesar (cf. below Pliny's Gene*sara*). In Strabo's *Geography*, he likewise connects the lake with the fertile plain: "the lake called Gennesar" (Strabo *Geog.* 16.2.16). Pliny preserves the same identification for the lake: "[The river Jordan] widens out into a lake usually called Genesara" (Pliny *Nat. Hist.* 5.71). He continues in his description but confuses Taricheae with Tiberias in identifying the lake: "Taricheae on the south, the name of which place some people give to the lake, and Tiberias on the west.…"

It is uncertain precisely when the lake began to be identified with the alluvial plain where Nahal 'Amud empties into the lake. Josephus reports on the advances of the Hasmonean forces there: "Jonathan set out from Galilee from *the waters of Gennesar*" (*Ant.* 13:158). Josephus' information is derived from 1 Maccabees 11:67: "Jonathan and his army encamped by the waters of Gennesar." Not only do the two accounts describe the same campaign, but these are the only two occasions where the term "the waters" is used with Gennesar to identify the lake.

The meaning of the place name is questioned as early as *Genesis Rabbah* 98:17 (ed. Albeck, 1267): "And why is it called Genosar? The Sages say [it means] 'the Gardens of the Princes.'" While the etymology of the toponym is addressed, the identity of the *Princes* (*sarim*) is not. David Flusser traced the use of *sar* during the days of the Hasmoneans and their consolidation of political rule in the second century B.C. In 1 Maccabees we read the acclamation in Jerusalem regarding Simon: "The Jews and their priests have resolved that Simon should be their *leader* and high priest forever, until a trustworthy prophet should arise" (1 Macc 14:41; cf. 13:42; 13:53; 14:35).

Flusser suggested that the linguistic equivalent for the Greek term translated leader should be the Hebrew *sar*. This is supported by the supposed Hebrew title for the First Book of Maccabees, "the Book of the Dynasty (*beit sar*) of the Sons of God" (Eus. *Hist. eccl.* 6.25.2), which presents the history of the Hasmoneans until the death of John Hyrcanus in 104 B.C. As Josephus reports, the son of Hyrcanus, Aristobulus I (104–103 B.C.), was the first of the Hasmoneans to "assume the diadem" (*J.W.* 1:70). Alexander Jannaeus (103–76 B.C.) followed his brother's example and minted coins with a bilingual inscription: "Yohanathan the King (in Hebrew) / King Alexander (in Greek)" (cf. *Ant.* 13:320).

Thus, it appears that among the Hasmonean rulers the title *sar* was applied for only a brief period, until the time of Aristobulus I. Thus, it seems that agricultural lands on the fertile plain belonging to Simon or John Hyrcanus

The Plain of Gennesaret with the Sea of Galilee in background, looking northeast. (photo S. Magal)

(the *sarim*) became the source for the toponym Gennesar. Subsequently, the region gave its name to the lake that adjoined it.

Among the Evangelists, Luke alone employs the toponym for the lake that Josephus states was used by those living in the region: "While the people pressed upon him to hear the word of God, he was standing by the lake of Gennesaret" (Luke 5:1). Luke studiously avoids the application of the term *thalassa* (i.e., sea) used by Matthew, Mark and John for the lake. The Greek term *thalassa* (like its Latin equivalent *mare*) typically describes brackish water; whereas, *limne* (and the Latin *lacus*) is routinely applied to fresh water. Thus, we have witnessed the consistent use of *limne* and *lacus* by the classical writers in connection with the Lake of Gennesar.

Matthew (14:22–33, 15:29, 17:27) and Mark (6:45–52, 7:31) use *thalassa* for the lake when there are no parallel passages in Luke. More often, however, we witness triple tradition narratives (Matt 4:18–22/Mark 1:16–20=Luke 5:1–11; Matt 8:23–27/Mark 4:35–41=Luke 8:22–25; Matt 8:28–34/Mark 5:1–20=Luke 8:26–39; Matt 13:1/Mark 4:1=Luke 8:4; cf. Mark 2:13=Luke 5:27; Mark 3:7=Luke 6:17) in which Luke's omission of *sea* and/or the correct use of *lake* suggests Lukan independence. Luke shows no reluctance to use the term *sea* at other times (Luke 17:2, 17:6, 21:25; Acts 4:2, 7:46 *et passim*). Whether Luke corrects Mark and Matthew on these occasions or draws his information from elsewhere, what is clear is that Luke presents a more informed picture of the physical nature of the lake.

Hasmonean coins of (above) John Hyrcanus and (below) Alexander Jannaeus.

We are still left with the unusual application of the term *sea* by Matthew, Mark and John to the Lake of Gennesar, and the related question of the origins for the Christian toponym the Sea of Galilee (Matt 4:18, 15:29; Mark 1:16, 7:31; John 6:1). The name Sea of Kinneret for the lake occurs three times in the Hebrew Scriptures (Num 34:11; Josh 12:3, 13:27) and is rendered by the Septuagint the Sea of Xenereth (or Xenera). Clearly, the translators have employed the term sea under the influence of the Hebrew *yam* that can designate either a lake or sea. The Aramaic Targums render the three biblical occurrences with the toponym the Sea of Gennesar. On two additional occasions where the lake is understood but the toponym Sea of Kinneret is lacking in the Hebrew texts, the Targums supply Lake of Gennesar. In Deuteronomy 33:23 "the lake and the south" is rendered "the Sea of Gennesar and south of it"; and again "east of the sea" in Ezekiel 39:11 is understood "east of the Sea of Gennesar."

Some scholars suggest that Matthew, Mark and John have derived their use of sea directly from the Septuagintal translation of the Sea of Kinneret. Yet, this is not certain. Why would the Evangelists not also have preserved the equally important Septuagintal qualifiers Xenereth or Xenera? Moreover, the Septuagint's rendering of the Sea of Kinneret provides no explanation for the New Testament use of *Galilee* with *sea*.

Instead, the genesis for the Christian toponym may be indicated by Matthew's scriptural citation immediately prior to his first use of the *Sea of Galilee*.

> He withdrew into Galilee; and leaving Nazareth he went and dwelt in Capernaum by the sea, in the territory of Zebulun and Naphtali, that what was spoken by the prophet Isaiah might be fulfilled: land of Zebulun and land of Naphtali, the way to the sea, along the Jordan, Galilee of the Gentiles—the people living in darkness have seen a great light; on those living in the land of the shadow of death a light has dawned. (Matt 4:12b–16)

Matthew cites Isaiah 9:1 (HMT 8:23) to interpret Jesus' movement in Galilee from Nazareth to Capernaum as a fulfillment of Old Testament prophecy.

Before we address Matthew's use of Isaiah, a few comments on the Hebrew passage are necessary. Anson F. Rainey is correct that *galil* in Isaiah 9:1 should not be read "Galilee" but "region". The name *Gelil-ha-goiim* designates the same area as Harosheth-ha-goiim in the Book of Judges: "from Harosheth-ha-goiim to the river Kishon" (Judg 4:13; cf. 4:2, 4:16). In other words, *Gelil-ha-goiim* refers to the arable lands (likely in the possession of non-Israelites) in the southern portions of the Jezreel Valley.

The tripartite topographical combination by Isaiah—"Way to the Sea," "Gelil-ha-goiim" and

JESUS' TRAVELS IN THE DISTRICTS OF TYRE AND CAESAREA PHILIPPI

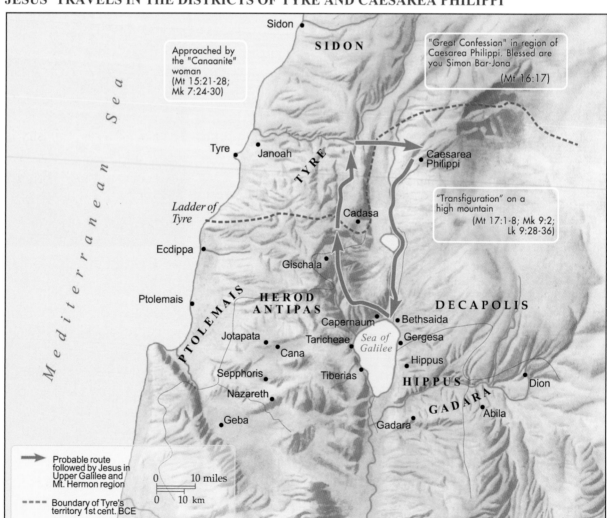

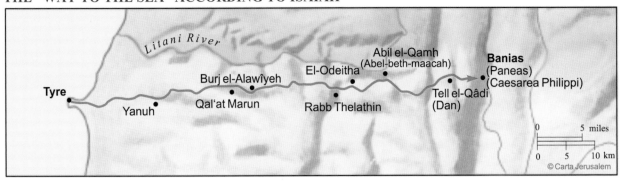

"Beyond the Jordan"—was intended by the prophet to define the frontiers of Israelite settlement in the north that stood in imminent danger before the Assyrian threat. Accordingly, the lands included "beyond the Jordan" marked the eastern frontier in the Transjordan, and "Gelil-ha-goiim" the southern boundaries of these northern settlements. In this context, Rainey is surely correct that Isaiah did not intend to identify "the way to the sea" with the international route from Egypt to Damascus, but the northern trunk route from Tyre to the region near the biblical city of Dan, i.e., Paneas (Banias).

Isaiah's intentions notwithstanding, Matthew took advantage of the Septuagint's rendering of the common noun *galil* to read Galilee. Further, the Evangelist collapsed the three widely divergent points of geographical reference to a single topos—the region around Capernaum that served as the locus for Jesus' ministry. So compelling was the early Christian exegesis preserved in Matthew's Gospel that it gave rise in subsequent centuries to the mistaken notion that the "Way to the Sea" traversed the region of Galilee near Capernaum.

Matthew's creative combination of geographical sites to define the locus of Jesus' ministry is clear. What is not so immediately recognizable is that this same creative exegesis is responsible for the Christian toponym, Sea of Galilee. In the entirety of Hebrew Scripture only in Isaiah 9:1 do we witness the collocation of the Hebrew terms *sea* and Galilee (i.e., *galil*). It seems that Matthew's citation was also intended to serve in the creation of a distinctive toponym within the early Christian community. Drawing upon the Septuagintal vocabulary of Isaiah 9:1 (*sea* and *Galilee*), the early Church created a new toponym that provided an elliptical allusion to Isaiah's prophecy and underscored the biblical significance of the locus of Jesus' ministry. If our observation is correct, we can now understand how the term *sea*—which in the Septuagint's translation of Isaiah initially spoke of the Mediterranean Sea—was transferred to another body of water, namely the Lake of Gennesar.

Mark embraced this Christian toponym (Mark 1:16, 3:7). Yet, he may provide some hint that he was also familiar with the location of Isaiah's earlier topographical points of reference. In Mark's account of Jesus' journey to the north he records, "Then Jesus left the vicinity of Tyre and went through Sidon, down to the Sea of Galilee and into the region of the Decapolis" (Mark 7:39). At a later point we will address more fully Mark's problematic use of Decapolis. For our purposes, it is sufficient to note that Mark's description of the beginning and end of Jesus' northern journey necessarily placed him on Isaiah's original "way to the sea", the trunk route from Tyre to Dan-Paneas-Caesarea Philippi (Mark 8:27; Matt 16:13). Moreover, it is only fitting that the destination of this journey according to Mark was the Sea of Galilee, whose very name was derived from the same Isaianic verse.

Once again it should be noted that Luke, while familiar with current redemptive notions attached to Isaiah 9:1 (e.g., Luke 1:79), betrays no knowledge of this Christian toponymic invention. We have already witnessed that he avoids the other Evangelists' use of *thalassa*, preferring instead the more correct *limne*. Luke's preference to apply *limne* to the Lake of Gennesar is also contrary to his often-assumed stylistic penchant to imitate the Septuagint, where *limne* appears infrequently (only five times in comparison to 432 occurrences of *thalassa*) and never for the Lake of Gennesar. His further omission of the Christian toponym strengthens the impression that he is relying here on other independent sources. Otherwise, it is difficult to explain how Luke could be drawing the topographical framework for his narrative from Mark or Matthew, while consistently and inexplicably omitting their key terminology.

What we witness in the Gospel traditions is the development of an early Christian toponym. The impetus for this creativity was to define the locus of Jesus' ministry in the regions of first-century Galilee in light of Isaiah 9:1. On the other hand, Luke's topographical independence is attested by his exclusive use of *limne* for the lake and his ignorance of the Christian place name. It may be significant that he likewise betrays no knowledge of the toponyms Gethsemane and Golgotha. He has instead drawn from sources that do not reflect the topographical creativity of Matthew, Mark or John. While his information possessed an intimate, firsthand knowledge of the physical nature of the lake, it does not reflect the spiritual environment that gave rise to the Christian toponym, *Sea of Galilee*.

Caesarea Philippi (Paneas). (photo S. Magal)

CHAPTER 5

THE FIRST CENTURY ENVIRONS OF THE SEA OF GALILEE

E VENTS RECORDED IN THE MINISTRY OF JESUS outside of Jerusalem are primarily located in the region around the Sea of Galilee, specifically in the north and northwest area of the lake. The Gospels are an important historical witness for Jewish settlement in this region. Scholarship seldom notes that for many of these settlements, their first mention in the literary witnesses is in the New Testament. After a confrontation in the synagogue in Nazareth, his boyhood home, Jesus relocated to Capernaum on the Sea of Galilee (Matt 4:13; Mark 1:21; Luke 4:31). This village would become the center of his ministry in the region. We now turn our attention to settlements around the Sea of Galilee that find mention in the New Testament.

Tiberias. It is no accident that the New Testament lacks a report of a visit by Jesus to Tiberias. Indeed, the city finds mention only in the Fourth Gospel (John 6:1, 6:23, 21:1) to designate the lake and to describe boats embarking from its port to bring people to Jesus. As Josephus reports, Herod Antipas founded the new capital of Galilee but took insufficient care with the placement of the city. He built it on an old cemetery, rendering all who dwelt there ritually defiled (Ant. 18:36–38). Josephus' description of those who settled in Tiberias is less than complimentary, and he states that Antipas even had to force some to reside in the new regional capital.

> The new settlers were a promiscuous rabble, no small contingent being Galilaean, with such as were drafted from territory subject to [Antipas] and brought forcibly to the new foundation. Some of these were magistrates. Herod accepted as participants even poor men who were brought in to join the others from any and all places of origin. (Ant. 18:37)

It is suggested that the city was founded in A.D. 18, although the coins of Antipas from Tiberias begin only from A.D. 20. In any event, it was not until the second century that Tiberias was purified under the direction of Simeon bar Yohai to render it fit for a religiously observant population (Gen. Rab. 79h; y. Shabb. 9, 1–38d). In the late Roman and Byzantine periods it became a center of Jewish learning and the location for the compilation of the Jerusalem Talmud.

Antipas selected the site because of its location on the shores of the Sea of Galilee. It benefited from the economy of the lake and its accessibility to nearby trade routes. It also is near the warm springs of Hammath (*Ant.* 18:36; *Life* 85; *J.W.* 2:614; cf. Pliny *Nat. Hist.* 5, 71; *Mo'ed Qat.* 18a; *y. Meg.* 2:1–2), a site already settled before Tiberias. Until recently the ancient remains of Tiberias lay beneath the modern city, and only meager finds from first-century Tiberias were known. Excavations in 1973–1974 unearthed a large structure that belonged to the time of Antipas. Archaeologists identified it as the gate complex belonging to the southern entrance to Tiberias. Renewed work in 2002 discovered a large wall—9 meters wide and 2 meters high. The excavators have suggested that it was a public building, perhaps the stadium mentioned by Josephus (*J.W.* 2:618; 3:539). The place of prayer, *proseuche* (*Life* 277, 280, 293), described by the historian in Tiberias, has yet to be found. In fact, the precise sense of this term for Josephus is unclear. Although he mentions a large building (*Life* 277) for the location of the proseuche where the public gathered in Tiberias, he does not otherwise use the term in such a way that it necessitates the meaning of a fixed structure (*J.W.* 5:388; *Ant.* 14:258). His citation from *Apion* describes prayers at Heliopolis offered in open-air (*Ag. Ap.* 2:10). The Greek term shares the same breadth of meaning in the New Testament (cf. Acts 16:13, 16:16).

Josephus mentions also a palace built by Antipas that was gilded with gold and decorated with "figures of living creatures" (*Life* 65–66). The tetrarch's transgression of Jewish law later contributed to the building's destruction. As we noted above, it may have been at the palace in Tiberias that Antipas gave a banquet on his birthday, "for his courtiers and officers and the leading men of Galilee" (Mark 6:21). Events at that banquet led to the Baptist's tragic end.

The city of Tiberias, looking southeast. (photo S. Ben-Yosef)

Magdala-Taricheae. At the foot of the Mount Arbel cliffs, on the road from Tiberias along the lakeshore, lay the settlement of Magdala. Its Hebrew and Greek names, Migdal-Nunia ("fish tower"; cf. *b. Pesah.* 46b) and Taricheae ("salted fish"; *Life* 188) reflect the dominant local industry of the first century. According to Strabo, "At the place called Taricheae the lake supplies excellent fish for pickling, and on its banks grow fruit-bearing trees resembling apple trees (Strabo *Geog.* 16.2.45).

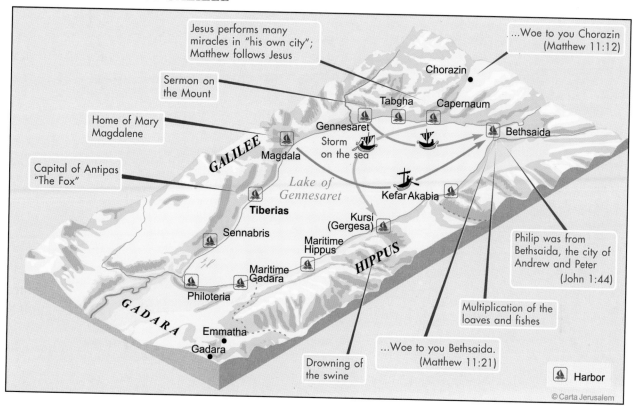

Apart from a poorly attested reading of Matthew 11:39, no mention is made of Jesus' presence at Magdala (cf. Mark 8:10). We likewise do not hear that any of the disciples come from here. Yet, Jesus' embarkation on a fishing boat from the plain of Gennesaret (Luke 5:1) would have brought him near to the tower of Magdala, which gave the town its name and where local fish were dried and salted. The only undisputed reference in the New Testament to Magdala is as the home of Mary Magdalene. She was among the women who followed Jesus from Galilee (Matt 27:56; John 19:25) and also with those who discovered Jesus' empty tomb (Luke 24:10).

Excavations since 2009 have uncovered houses, streets, ritual immersion baths and the ancient harbor of Magdala from the Hasmonean and Roman periods. Of particular note is a monumen-

tal structure that the archaeologists have identified as the first-century synagogue. It was decorated with mosaics and frescoes and included an ornately incised limestone table, one of the finest examples of stonework ever discovered from the days of the Second Temple.

Travel between Tiberias and Magdala is described both in rabbinic literature

Ornately decorated limestone artifact, from the remains of a first-century synagogue at Magdala.
(photo R. S. Notley)

33

(left) A first-century mikveh uncovered in the recent excavations at Magdala-Taricheae. Excavators claim that it is the only "self-filling" mikveh found in the country because of the water table underneath that keeps it filled. If one empties it, in ten minutes the mikveh is full again. (photo R. S. Notley)

(below) A view of the secondary use of stones and column drums to block up the streets. Excavators suggest that this is what is indicated by Josephus "fortifying Magdala." (photo R. S. Notley)

and Josephus, who speaks of "a road to Taricheae, which is thirty furlongs [c. 3.5 mi./5 km] distant from Tiberias" (Life 157). His description is to be preferred over Pliny's placement of Taricheae, south of the Sea of Galilee, "Taricheae on the south (a name which is by many persons given to the lake itself), and of Tiberias on the west" (Pliny Nat. Hist. 5:15).

Josephus presents Taricheae as the center of its own toparchy in A.D. 54, when it was awarded by Nero to Agrippa II. Together with the toparchy of Tiberias, Taricheae comprised eastern Galilee (J.W. 2:252). The historian, who was given the responsibility for the defense of Galilee, includes Taricheae in a list of cities of Lower Galilee that he fortified in preparation for the war with Rome (Life 188; 156). Evidence of Josephus' fortification of Taricheae has been discovered, but there has not been certain identification of the *proseuche* (Life 280) or hippodrome (J.W. 2:599). He describes a sea-battle at Taricheae that resulted in a devastating Jewish loss. Residents fled to Tiberias thinking they would not be able to return. It may be that Taricheae was absorbed into Tiberias after the Jewish Revolt.

Capernaum. Our most plentiful literary witness to the village of Capernaum is the New Testament. Jesus moved to Capernaum after his rejection in Nazareth (Matt 4:13), and it was subsequently known as "his own city" (Matt 9:1). A number of Jesus' disciples were chosen there (Matt 4:13–22, 8:5–22, 9:1–34; Mark 1:21–34, 2:1–17; Luke 7:1–10), and he is reported to preach in the synagogue on more than one occasion (Luke 4:31; John 6:59). Jesus is also found in the home of Peter, which is described in Capernaum (Luke 4:38).

The only other first-century witness to Capernaum comes from Josephus. He reports that he was carried to the village of Capernaum when he was wounded in battle near Bethsaida (*Life* 403). Otherwise, his only reference to the town is in his description of the western region of the Lake of Gennesar. It is the first-century eyewitness description that challenged nineteenth-century explorers, who desired to rediscover this important city from the Gospels. After describing the fruitfulness of the plain of Gennesar, Josephus continues,

> ...besides being favored by its genial air, the country is watered by a highly fertilizing spring, called by the inhabitants Capharnaum; some have imagined this is to be a branch of the Nile, from its producing a fish resembling the coracin found in the lake of Alexandria. The region [i.e., Gennesar] extends along the border of the lake that bears its name for a length of thirty furlongs and inland to a depth of twenty. Such is the nature of this district. (*J.W.* 3:519–521)

According to his description, the region that coursed along the northwest edge of the lake was known as Gennesar, and within its limits was an area of springs known by the name Capernaum. The historian makes no mention of a village in his description, perhaps an unconscious omission because his attention was focused on the natural surroundings.

Nevertheless, what early explorers found most puzzling was the mention of the springs of Capernaum. Those familiar with today's setting of Capernaum, recognize that within the vicinity of the site there are no springs. Instead, 3 miles (5 km) to the west are springs known locally as Tabgha, a corruption of its Greek name Heptapegon (i.e., seven springs).

Prior to modern exploration, the first Christian pilgrim to record their visit was Egeria (c. fifth century A.D.). Her itinerary is preserved in the writings of Peter the Deacon. Egeria was followed

Capernaum: remains of the synagogue, 3rd to 4th centuries A.D. (photo S. Magal)

Capernaum: the so-called House of St. Peter. An octagonal church was built upon the site, with a glass floor to view the ancient remains below.
(photo S. Magal)

three centuries later by Bishop Arculf (c. A.D. 700). He described his visit to Capernaum, not a great distance beyond "where the loaves were blessed" (i.e., Tabgha).

Only a few years later (c. A.D. 724), he was followed by Willibald, who traveled in the same direction as Egeria and Arculf, leaving north from Tiberias along the shore of the lake. Two details from Willibald's journal are important for our consideration. First, he describes Capernaum with a great wall, while Arculf is explicit that the village had no walls. Further, Willibald relates that in Capernaum he was shown the house of "Zebedaeus with his sons John and James," while in Bethsaida he saw a church on the place of Peter and Andrew's house. While Willibald may have confused Capernaum for Bethsaida, he is in agreement with Arculf in his omission of a church at Capernaum in his day.

Modern archaeological excavations at Capernaum have uncovered a city laid out with a Hippodamian (orthogonal) street plan. Several insulae-style houses have been uncovered and partially restored. Excavators have determined that resettlement of the city began in the Persian period and grew throughout the Hellenistic and Roman periods. It fell into disrepair and was abandoned during the Islamic invasion in the seventh century A.D. This state of affairs fits the description of the eighth-century visitors to Capernaum.

Two structures have drawn considerable attention. As we have noted, Byzantine Christian pilgrims were shown a church built upon the house of Peter. Excavations have uncovered a series of sanctuaries that likely correspond to these testimonies. Archaeologists suggest that the beginnings of veneration for this location began in a *domus ecclesia*. Epiphanius records that Joseph of Tiberias was authorized by the emperor Constantine to build the church in Capernaum (Epiph. *Adv. haer.* 30.4.1). The archaeological evidence suggests that the earlier house was transformed into a church, and it is likely this structure that Egeria visited in the early fifth century A.D. In the second half of the fifth century an octagonal church was erected. As we have noted, the testimony of the eighth-century pilgrimage to Capernaum may indicate that the church no longer existed at this time.

The synagogue of Capernaum that dates to the fourth or fifth century is built in an early Galilean

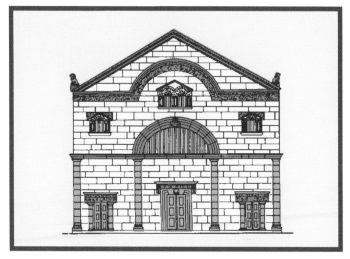

style and is the largest synagogue discovered in the Land of Israel. It was first partially excavated by Kohl and Watzinger. Their efforts were later followed by the Franciscan custody of the Holy Land. Two synagogues have been identified on the same location. The later limestone synagogue is the one visited by Egeria, who describes its many steps and cut stones. Forming the foundation of the Byzantine synagogue are the remains of walls from what is proposed to be an earlier synagogue, perhaps dating to the first century A.D. This structure would then be the synagogue mentioned in the Gospels in which Jesus taught.

Finally, a malediction by Rabbi Issi in the third century A.D. against the heretics of Capernaum indicates that Judeo-Christians lived among the Jewish community of Capernaum in the late Roman period. Indeed, Epiphanius testifies that still in the fourth century A.D. among the Jewish communities of "Tiberias, Diocaesarea, also called Sepphoris, Nazareth, and Capernaum they take care to have no foreigners living among them" (Epiph. *Adv. haer.* 30.11.10). The continuance of an observant Jewish community in the Byzantine period in Capernaum may also be indicated by the discovery of a sixth-century A.D. Aramaic inscription in the floor of the synagogue at Hammath Gader, which mentions a donor named Yosse bar Dosti of Capernaum.

The historical and material witness of the community at Capernaum serves as a caution against the premature imposition by scholars of "the parting of the ways" upon Judaism and Christianity uniformly at an early period. At Capernaum and elsewhere in Roman-Byzantine Palestine, the archaeological evidence points to coexistence. At a minimum, the evidence adds further challenge to the erroneous assumption that the *Birkhat ha-Minnim* in its earliest form expressed Jewish antipathy towards nascent Christianity.

Chorazin. Of the three Galilean cities (Capernaum, Chorazin and Bethsaida) Jesus mentions as places in which he performed miracles (Matt 11:21; Luke 10:13), only Chorazin is not located on the Sea of Galilee. It is about 2 miles (3 km) north of Capernaum on the basalt slopes of the Rosh Pinna sill and near the Ptolemais–Bethsaida road that crosses the Jordan River. According to Jewish sources, the wheat from this town (t. *Mak.* 3:8) was of exceptional quality (b. *Menah.* 85a). Chorazin flourished in the second century A.D., likely as a result of the increase of the Jewish population in Galilee in the aftermath of the Bar Kokhba rebellion (A.D. 132–135).

The archaeological evidence indicates that the town suffered a devastating earthquake in the early fourth century A.D., but was rebuilt and continued to exist into the Byzantine period. This stands at odds with Eusebius' description at the beginning of the fourth century A.D. that Chorazin was already an abandoned village. "Chorazin. A village in Galilee. Christ cursed it according to

Remains of the basalt synagogue at Chorazin, late Roman period. (photo S. Magal)

the Gospel. Now it is a deserted place two miles from Capernaum" (Eus. *Onom.* 174:23).

A Dutch officer, C. W. M. Van de Velde, who traveled in the Near East in the mid-nineteenth century, first identified the site of Khirbet Karazzeh with Chorazin. Kohl and Watzinger later included the synagogue of Chorazin in their survey of synagogues in Galilee. More recent excavations have uncovered houses and a ritual bathing installation. Nevertheless, only a small portion of the site has been excavated, and first-century Chorazin has yet to be identified.

Chorazin's late Roman period synagogue is in early Galilean style, similar to those at Capernaum and Bar'am. Excavators have also found ornamental fragments belonging to the synagogue's Torah ark, where the congregation's scrolls were kept, and the platform (*bema*) on which the Torah would have been read on the Sabbath and other appointed days.

The Search for Bethsaida. One of the challenging tasks for archaeologists and biblical historians alike is the identification of sites mentioned in the Bible, some of which were destroyed or disappeared in time without a trace. The first comprehensive attempt to locate these places was that of Eusebius, the fourth-century church historian (c. A.D. 260–339). In his *Onomasticon* Eusebius catalogued most of the cities, sites and regions mentioned in the Old and New Testaments. Supplementing his list when possible, Eusebius provided detailed information concerning the sites' history and location, including their distances in Roman miles from other well-known metropolitan centers in fourth-century Palestine.

Although the scale of Eusebius' compilation is impressive, the work's most glaring failure is his reliance upon the Septuagint, whose translators at times did not fully understand the meaning of the Hebrew terminology in the Old Testament. Eusebius and the Septuagintal text on which he depends occasionally mistake a common noun, adjective or adverb in Hebrew for a place name. By so doing, the *Onomasticon* presents ninety place names—almost ten percent of the total listed—of sites that never existed.

At other times, the brevity of Eusebius' descriptions—with nothing more than the barest details taken from the biblical text—suggests that the location of the site was already lost by the time of his writing at the beginning of the fourth century. This seems to be the case with Bethsaida, one of the cities mentioned in connection with the ministry of Jesus (Matt 11:21; Luke 10:13). Eusebius reports: "The city of Andrew and Peter and Philip. It is located in Galilee next to the lake of Gennesaret." Eusebius received his information about Bethsaida from the tradition of the Fourth Gospel that it was the home of Philip, Andrew and Peter (John 1:44), and "in Galilee" (John 12:21).

He adopted the detail that the village was "next to the lake of Gennesaret" *verbatim* from the description of Josephus (*Ant.* 18:28). Elsewhere Eusebius credits Josephus by name (cf. Eus. *Onom.* 1:2=Ant. 1:92–95; Eus. *Onom.* 40:9=Ant. 1:118; Eus. *Onom.* 82:2=Ant. 1:147). Since Eusebius only repeats details about Bethsaida found in well-known first-century sources, and he himself supplies no additional physical description, it is likely that by his own day the hometown of the three apostles had been abandoned and its location forgotten. Other deserted biblical sites—which amounted to little more than visible piles of ruins in the fourth century—are described as such by Eusebius (cf. Chorazin: Eus. *Onom.* 174:23). The absence of physical details concerning Bethsaida seems to indicate that our New Testament city had disappeared entirely.

Edward Robinson.

Bethsaida was lost for centuries, and its location the subject of speculation by pilgrims and map-makers. With the advent of geographical exploration of the Holy Land in the nineteenth century, the search intensified in the northern regions of the Sea of Galilee. Two theories put forward during that time still dominate the debate today. Edward Robinson in 1838 was the first to suggest that et-Tell—the location of the present-day Bethsaida Excavations Project—was the site of ancient Bethsaida-Julias. Later, a German explorer, Gottlieb Schumacher, citing the problem of et-Tell's distance from the lake, proposed an alternative site at el-Araj—today located on lands maintained by the Israel Nature Reserves Authority.

Although never excavated, el-Araj was still advanced by the late Mendel Nun of Kibbutz 'En Gev as the possible site of Bethsaida. His identification was bolstered by a survey of el-Araj in 1991 under the auspices of the Israel Antiquities Authority that found Roman period surface remains. These initial findings were confirmed in May 2014 in a shovel survey carried out under the direction of Mordechai Aviam and Dina Shalem. The pottery remains indicate that el-Araj was a Jewish village that existed from at least the early Hellenistic (Hasmonean) period into the Byzantine period. This profile is what one would expect for the site of New Testament Bethsaida.

Nevertheless, today for Christian visitors to the Holy Land, the debate seems a foregone conclusion. Et-Tell is identified both on Israel government maps and road signs as "Bethsaida." Yet, have twenty-five years of excavations by the Bethsaida Excavations Project (BEP) at et-Tell demonstrated beyond reasonable doubt that it was the site of ancient Bethsaida? Nagging questions remain. True, it is rare that archaeology can prove with absolute certainty the identity of a particular site. Recent exceptions are Tel Miqne (Ekron) and Tell el-Qâdī (Dan), where inscriptions found at those sites identified them as the ancient biblical cities. More often, however, the task of site identification is the complex application of multiple disciplines: history, toponymy, topography and archaeology.

While there are limits to the certainty of conclusions based solely on archaeological excavations, they can serve in another way—to eliminate mistaken identification. If multiple, independent and reliable historical sources indicate human settlement during a particular period, and archaeological investigation on a site finds no corresponding material remains that correlate to that historical period, then the paucity of the evidence should bring into question the identification of the site. In this brief survey we want to examine the ancient historical descriptions of Bethsaida and inquire whether the ancient portrait of Bethsaida corresponds to the discoveries of recent excavations at et-Tell.

The oldest historical references to Bethsaida are those found in the New Testament. As we have noted, it was one of the Galilean cities where Jesus ministered. Here Mark records that Jesus healed a blind man (Mark 8:22). It is also the region where Jesus withdrew on more than one occasion: "On their return the apostles told him what they had done. And he took them and withdrew apart (i.e., by boat: Mark 6:32) to a city called Bethsaida" (Luke 9:10; cf. Mark 6:45).

Apart from the New Testament our most abundant witness for first-century Bethsaida is that of Josephus. He includes the city in his description of the course of the Jordan River that "traverses another hundred and twenty furlongs (i.e., 15 mi./24 km beyond Lake Semechonitis), and after the city of Julias (Bethsaida) cuts across the Lake of Gennesar" (J.W. 3:515). Of Herod Philip's efforts at Bethsaida Josephus reports,

> He raised the village of Bethsaida on Lake Gennesaret to the status of city (i.e., *polis*) by adding residents and strengthening the fortifications. He named it after Julia, the emperor's daughter. (*Ant.* 18:28; *J.W.* 2:168)

Josephus' testimony is the only record that Philip renamed the village of Bethsaida as Julias.

The northern shore of the Sea of Galilee and the plain of Bethsaida, looking east. (photo A. Alon)

He is likewise alone in his explanation that the city was
named for Julia, the daughter of Augustus (*Ant.* 18:28; *J.W.* 2:168).
The historian may have confused the identity of Julia. The
daughter of Augustus was banished in 2 B.C., while Livia, the
second wife of the emperor, was granted Julian *gens* in his
will, which was executed at his death in A.D. 14. It is doubtful
Philip would have begun his initiatives at Bethsaida in the
first two years of his rule (4–2 B.C.). It is likewise difficult to
imagine the tetrarch dedicating the city to Augustus' daughter
after her banishment in 2 B.C. A coin found recently inscribed
to the widow of Augustus—Julia Sebaste—was minted by

Coin of Agrippa II (A.D. 50–100).

Philip and dated to A.D. 30/31. It thus seems that the Julia to whom Josephus refers in the renaming
of Bethsaida was Livia-Julia, wife of Augustus and mother of Tiberius.

Josephus reports that Philip died at Bethsaida-Julias. "He died at Julias; and when he was carried
to that monument which he had already erected for himself beforehand, he was buried with great
pomp" (*Ant.* 18:106–108). Although it is often assumed that Philip's mausoleum was at Bethsaida-Julias, this detail is not actually stated by Josephus. The proximity of Josephus' reference to Philip's
death and his burial need not indicate proximity in location. The death and burial of Philip's father
illustrates this point (cf. *J.W.* 1:670–673). The location of Philip's tomb remains unknown.

Early in the Jewish Revolt, the marshy plain near Bethsaida was the location of fighting between
Jewish forces led by Josephus and the troops under the command of the Roman Sulla (*Life* 399).
Josephus' horse stumbled on the marshy land and fell, injuring its rider. He escaped, only to sur-
render a short time later at Jotapata (*J.W.* 3:316–339). Josephus' topographical details of the skirmish
between his forces and those of Agrippa II with the description that his encampment was near the
Jordan River and "as far as the plain," presupposes a plain between et-Tell and the lake, so that the
lake at the time of Josephus did not by any means reach as far as et-Tell.

Finally, a brief comment is warranted concerning the anachronistic toponym, Bethsaida of Galilee in the Fourth Gospel (John 12:21). This unfortunate designation has been the genesis of futile
searches for a western Bethsaida and even two Bethsaidas. Yet, the regional qualifier (i.e., of
Galilee) should be read only as a chronological marker for the historical context of the Evangelist.
Changes in regional terminology may have resulted from the consolidation of political power by
Agrippa I or Agrippa II on both sides of the upper Jordan River, or even more likely from geopolitical changes by the Romans after the Jewish Revolt (A.D. 66–70).

Subsequent to the Jewish Revolt, Pliny and Ptolemy join the Evangelist in speaking of territory
east of the Jordan River as Galilee. The region of Galilee no longer marked the frontiers of political
power on the western side of the upper Jordan River. Nonetheless, these later developments in no
way reflect the terminological or political realities in the days of Jesus. During the rule of Antipas
and Philip, Bethsaida was not in Galilee.

With this short survey of the description of Bethsaida, we can now summarize what is known
about the city through the eyes of the ancient records.

• It was a fishing village that was transformed by Herod Philip into a Greco-Roman *polis* named
  Julias.

- Philip increased the population and strengthened the fortifications of the city.
- Bethsaida contained both Gentile (Syrian) and Jewish populations (*J.W.* 3:57; John 1:44). Among the latter were those who maintained a religiously observant lifestyle (cf. Acts 11:8).
- Accessible by boat (Mark 6:32), the city lay on the Sea of Galilee (*Ant.* 18:28).
- It was situated about 660 feet (200 m) from the Jordan River that coursed by it and emptied into the Sea of Galilee (*Life* 399).
- It was in lower Gaulanitis, opposite the higher hill country (*J.W.* 2:168).
- The area nearby included a marshy plain (*Life* 403).

The city underwent significant changes during the last two centuries of the Second Jewish Commonwealth. From a small thriving Jewish fishing village to a Greco-Roman *polis*, it increased in prominence and size. We are now left to ask, do the archaeological finds of twenty-five years of excavations at et-Tell correspond to the picture provided by those who knew Bethsaida-Julias firsthand?

The conclusions of the Bethsaida Excavations Project (BEP) are not always easy to assess. Over the years there have been varied and conflicting claims made by the excavators. In spite of the suggestion by the excavation's director, Rami Arav, that Bethsaida was destroyed and disappeared in the local fighting of A.D. 65–66, he does not provide any archaeological evidence for the destruction of Bethsaida during the Jewish Revolt. Nor is there any evidence of its destruction detailed in the volumes of the excavation report. Instead, in volume two another member of the excavation team—Heinz-Wolfgang Kuhn—concluded, that Bethsaida-Julias was still settled after the Jewish-Roman war (A.D. 66 to c. 74).

This assessment of the archaeological evidence concurs with numerous references to Bethsaida in early rabbinic literature. Together they present a strong argument that the city continued to exist after the Jewish Revolt. To the rabbinic witnesses should be added two pagan writers—Pliny the Elder (Pliny *Nat. Hist.* 5.71) and Ptolemy (Ptol. *Geog.* 5.15.3)—who both attest to the existence of Bethsaida after the Jewish Revolt.

It seems that Bethsaida was not a city familiar to the rabbis after approximately the third century A.D., which corresponds with Avi-Yonah's description of the regional decline of Jewish commu-

Remains of et-Tell, the recently proposed site of Bethsaida. (photo S. Magal)

nities in Roman Palestine in the third century. He explains that this occurred because of political and economic crises elsewhere in the empire.

His description explains the disappearance of Bethsaida as part of an overall decline in Jewish communities in Roman Palestine in the third century, beginning in the Golan and Bashan. It also accords with the disappearance of Bethsaida by the time of Eusebius' composition of the *Onomasticon* at the beginning of the fourth century A.D.

We now turn our attention to the two problems that run to the heart of the site identification of Bethsaida at et-Tell. The first is the distance of the site from the shores of the Sea of Galilee. Both the New Testament and Josephus describe Bethsaida near the lakeshore. Its very name means "place of fishing," and its reputation in the Tannaitic and Amoraic periods remained closely identified with the fishing industry. The location of et-Tell is

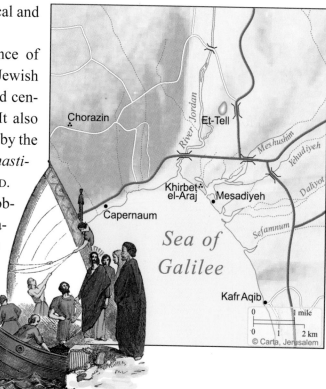

THE PLAIN OF BETHSAIDA

about 1.8 miles (3 km) from the lake, an unlikely setting for a fishing village. To overcome this challenge, the excavators theorize that et-Tell's current remoteness is the result of geological cataclysms and the silting of the Jordan River. According to a geological study of the area provided in the first and second excavation reports, the Bethsaida plain was underwater at some point between 2,700 and 1,800 years ago. Nevertheless, the challenge remains to demonstrate the particular pertinence of this nine-hundred-year span to our narrow window of historical interest in the early Roman period.

Moreover, all of the discussion of possible geological cataclysms has diverted attention from the real problem with the site identification of et-Tell as a first-century fishing village. Even if a catastrophic geological event could be identified which destroyed first-century Bethsaida-Julias, it would not solve et-Tell's topographical impediment to being the first-century fishing village *cum* Greco-Roman *polis*. The elevation at the base of the mound is too high.

Surveys around the Sea of Galilee have provided verifiable and objective data regarding the levels of the lake in the New Testament period. The present lake level averages 690 feet (210.5 m) below sea level. Its level today is about 3 feet (1 m) higher than in antiquity because of a modern-day dam that has raised the water level. The elevations of breakwaters and piers that belong to the sixteen first-century harbors around the lake support this contention.

Basalt blocks identified by the excavators as Bethsaida's "old dock facility" at the base of the tel are measured at an elevation of –669 feet/–204 meters. This is over 22 feet (7 m) higher than the first-century lake levels. If the BEP excavation report is correct and the lake reached what the excavators claim is the docking facility of first-century Bethsaida-Julias, then the lake

Remains of a Roman theater at Sepphoris, a feature usually found in a Greco-Roman polis. (photo S. Magal)

would have inundated the shoreline promenade at Capernaum (–686.5 ft./–209.25 m), the ports of Tiberias (–686.4 ft./–208.3 m) and Kursi (–686.5 ft./–209.25 m), and every other known first-century settlement around the lake.

Equally challenging is the near total absence of material remains from the early Roman (New Testament) period. Archaeological evidence indicates that et-Tell was a significant fortified city in the Iron Age. The archaeologists suggest it belonged to the kingdom of Geshur (2 Sam 3:3). A monumental gate complex faced east and was discovered together with cultic stelae and a basalt basin adjacent to the gate. The city was probably destroyed during the Assyrian invasion in the eighth century B.C. There is evidence of renewed settlement during the Persian period with a continuity of occupation into the Hellenistic period. The material remains from the earlier occupation stand in stark contrast to the Roman period. According to the published finds, the Hellenistic and Roman fineware from et-Tell ranges from 200 B.C. to 100 B.C., and rarely to the first century B.C.

These observations are consistent with the ceramic typology given in the second volume of the excavation report. The totals from the detailed tables of ceramic finds taken from areas A and B are as follows: 296 vessels from the Iron Age, 71 Hellenistic and 53 Roman. The decline is even more severe if one removes from consideration the remains from area A that we are told are comprised entirely of a pit filled with composite pottery. The distribution then is 294 vessels from the Iron Age, 51 Hellenistic and 13 Roman.

The report about coins found at et-Tell is likewise compelling and points us in the same direction as the ceramic evidence. There were 105 coins found minted in the Hellenistic period (333–63

B.C.); 9 Herodian (Herod I [1]; Antipas [1]; Archelaus [1]; Philip [3]; Agrippa I [1]; Agrippa II [2]); 16 Middle to Late Roman; 4 Byzantine; 64 Islamic (Umayyad, 19th century).

The distribution of fineware is consistent with the pottery, coins and structural remains and indicates a visible decline in the early Roman period. So, while today two large Hellenistic private homes are prominently displayed, only one small, poorly attested Roman period house is presented in the excavation reports. This poor state of affairs in the Roman period at et-Tell stands in irreconcilable conflict with the historical picture of first-century Bethsaida-Julias, when it is reported at its zenith in size and prominence.

It is precisely at this point in history that Josephus records that Herod Philip transformed the Jewish fishing village of Bethsaida into a Greco-Roman *polis*. To date there exists little if any evidence of the fortifications attributed by Josephus to Philip's enhancement of the city. Neither is there any identifiable structure from what one would expect of a Roman *polis*. The awarding of *polis* status upon a city was intended to introduce elements of Greco-Roman culture into Near Eastern societies. One would have expected to see some evidence of a theater (Tiberias, Sepphoris), gymnasium (Beth-shean), hippodrome (Sebaste, Caesarea), or other elements of Roman life introduced into Bethsaida-Julias.

We should quickly qualify these comments to say that hesitation by scholars who think that Josephus has exaggerated the extent of Philip's efforts may be correct. In their estimation, Julias never was a real *polis*. These questions notwithstanding, even if Josephus has exaggerated the size and significance of Bethsaida-Julias, this does not mitigate nor explain the near absence of material remains at et-Tell during Philip's rule. After over twenty years of excavations, the only structure of any significance that the excavators can point to is the foundation of what some—but not all—of the excavators suggest is a Roman temple.

According to the excavation report the evidence for its identification as a temple is: (1) the relative thickness of the walls in comparison to the average thickness of other structures at the site; (2) the "rough" east-west orientation of the rectangular structure; (3) a column foundation; (4) a porch *in antae* in both its east and west ends; (5) rooms that the excavators identify as the possible *pronaos* and *cella*.

In addition to these structural identifications, nearby were discovered an incense shovel and a clay female figurine. Some of the excavators have suggested that these two items were associated with the proposed temple and local imperial cult of Julia. Yet, there simply is not enough information to determine the shovel's date or to know whether it belonged to Jews or pagans. It certainly does not provide conclusive evidence of the presence of the imperial cult at et-Tell. Since there is no evidence of the shovel's actual usage, even less should it be used in an attempt to identify the nearby structure as a Roman temple.

Supporting evidence for the identification of the structure as a Roman temple is likewise inconclusive. It lacks any of the fine work one would have expected of a temple dedicated to Julias. A small threshold stone is the single dressed stone that was found at the site close to the *in situ* position. However, the excavators admit that even this stone is too small for "a main entrance."

A comparison with Roman temples in the Near East illustrates that et-Tell's putative temple is the only one of such rough and meager construction. The BEP excavators acknowledge this humble state of affairs in their comparison between their structure and Roman temples in the Hauran and

An incense shovel from the Roman period.

in northern Syria. Most of these are built of fine dressed stones and resemble only vaguely that found at et-Tell. They are forced to conclude that if this is a temple built by Philip the tetrarch in honor of Livia-Julia, it certainly was very modest next to those built by Philip's father in Samaria or Caesarea Maritima. The recent discovery of a nearby Roman period temple in the territory of Philip only heightens the qualitative disparity between the structure at et-Tell and other recognized Roman temples in the region.

The excavators from the Bethsaida Excavation Project have theorized that the reason we only find the temple's foundations and no dressed stones on the site is because the stones were taken and re-used in the synagogue of Chorazin. They provide only two pieces of evidence to support this exaggerated claim. First, the width of the Chorazin synagogue approximates that of their proposed Roman temple at et-Tell. Second, the excavators claim that an eagle in a frieze from the Chorazin synagogue is evidence that it originally belonged to a Roman structure, since the eagle was the symbol for Rome.

Their line of reasoning fails on both accounts. The width of the Chorazin synagogue is consistent with other undisputed Roman-Byzantine synagogues in the region. Thus, there is no necessary connection with the dimensions of the building foundations at et-Tell. Second, the eagle was a common motif found in the ornamentation of regional synagogues in late antiquity. Indeed, Herod already included the eagle in the decorations of the Jerusalem temple *(J.W.* 1:650–656; *Ant.* 17:149–163). Quite simply, there is no compelling evidence to support the excavators' suggestion that the missing temple of Bethsaida-Julias is to be found in the stones of the Chorazin synagogue. Further, the incongruity of the structure at et-Tell and other Roman temples in the region raises serious doubts whether the public building found at et-Tell was indeed a Roman temple to Livia-Julia.

Our survey of the ancient eyewitnesses and recent archaeological results from the Bethsaida Excavations Project leaves many unresolved questions. The evidence of over twenty-five years of excavations is far from conclusive in bolstering the claim that et-Tell is first-century Bethsaida-Julias. The site's remoteness from the lake, together with the inexplicable absence of first-century remains, challenges the identification of et-Tell with the lost city of Philip, Andrew and Peter. Certainly more investigation is needed. Perhaps future excavations at et-Tell or elsewhere in the vicinity will prove conclusive for the site identification of this important New Testament city, but for the time being, the location of ancient Bethsaida remains in question.

Gergesa. The reader of the Gospels is faced with a complex textual and topographical challenge in identifying the location of Jesus' encounter with the demoniac "on the other side opposite Galilee" (Matt 8:28–34; Mark 5:1–17; Luke 8:26–37).

In spite of the strong textual witnesses for either Gadara or Gerasa, geographers struggle with these settings because of the topographical problems they present. According to all of the accounts, Jesus' encounter followed a boat ride from Capernaum, during which there was a sudden and violent storm (Matt 8:23–27; Mark 7:35–41; Luke 8:22–25). Afterwards, Jesus and his disciples arrived to their destination, which is additionally described by Mark and Matthew as "the other side [of the sea]" (Matt 8:28; Mark 5:1). Typically in the New Testament "the other side" describes the northeast side of the lake opposite Capernaum and Gennesaret. In fact, on one occasion, Mark uses this same language and further specifies, "the other side, to Bethsaida" (Mark 6:45). Matthew and Mark's identification of the region corresponds to Luke's regional description, "opposite Galilee" (Luke 8:26).

Quite simply, neither Gadara nor Gerasa fits the description presented by the Gospels for the destination of Jesus' journey. Gadara (=Umm Qeis), the capital of a toparchy, was about six miles southeast of the Sea of Galilee, Gerasa (=Jerash, a city of Perea) about thirty-three miles. At such remote distances from the lake, these cities are not suitable candidates for the point of destination of a crossing of the Sea of Galilee from Capernaum.

It should be quickly added that the region of Gadara may likely have reached the southern shores of the lake. Coins of Gadara in the Roman period depict naval battles, suggesting that the district of Gadara extended to the lakeshore, where theatrical sea battles called "Naumachia" were held (e.g., Dio Cass. 43.23; Suet. *Jul.* 39; Suet. *Aug.* 43; Tac. *Ann.* 12.56, 14.15). During a drought in the 1980s, the low water level of the Sea of Galilee allowed investigation along the shoreline, which had been inundated in modern times because of a modern dam. Sixteen first-century harbors were identified around the

Chapel southeast of the basilica, 5th or 6th century, at Kursi, looking northwest toward the Sea of Galilee. The location of these remains on the slope may support the identification of the site with the locale of the miracle of the Gadarene swine. (photo S. Magal)

lake, including that of Gadara near Tell Samara on the southeastern shore of the Sea of Galilee.

The discovery of Gadara's harbor supports the statement of Josephus that the region of Gadara extended along the southern shores of the Sea of Galilee to the point where the Jordan River exited the lake on its southwestern end. The Jordan River north of the Sea of Galilee and its southern exit from the lake were points of demarcation for the eastern frontier of the region of Galilee: "[Justus] went out, and set the villages that belonged to Gadara and Hippus on fire; *which villages were situated on the borders of Tiberias*, and of the region of Scythopolis" (*Life* 42).

Mention of Tiberias should not be read "lake of Tiberias" (i.e., *J.W.* 3:57) but the capital of Galilee, as it appears in the following lines of Josephus' narrative (*Life* 43). The appearance of the city, similar to the mention of Scythopolis, is intended to signal the region about the city, in this instance Galilee. The historian's use of the region of Gadara to mark the limits of Galilee parallels a similar use of Gadara in his description of the borders of Galilee:

> On the south the country is bounded by Samaria and the territory of Scythopolis up to the waters of Jordan; on the east by the territory of Hippus, Gadara and Gaulanitis, the frontier-line of Agrippa's kingdom. (*J.W.* 3:37)

Nevertheless, while the toparchy of Gadara extended to the shores of the Sea of Galilee, its position was too far south for the event described in the Gospels.

In the investigation of the harbor of Gadara a large tower on the shoreline was discovered, which may have marked the northern frontiers of the city's territory. The limits of Gadara's shoreline are important, because there are no nearby slopes reaching the lake included in the region of Gadara that would fit the topographical description portrayed in the Gospel accounts: "The herd (of swine)

Area overlooking Hammath Gader (Umm Qeis) and the Yarmuk River, looking east. (photo S. Magal)

Beth-shean (Scythopolis): general view of the Greco-Roman remains. (photo S. Magal)

rushed *down the steep bank* into the lake and were drowned" (Luke 8:33; cf. Matt 8:32; Mark 5:13).

Already at the beginning of the third century A.D., Origen recognized the topographical problems of Gerasa and Gadara for our account. He offered a suggestion based on the topographical setting and local traditions: Gergesa, "an ancient city…by the lake now called Tiberias, by which is a cliff overhanging the lake, from which they show that the swine were cast down by the devils" (Origen *Comm. on John* 6:41). The site of this ancient village lies in the Wâdī Samekh delta just north of the only point at which the overlooking heights of Gaulanitis descend to the lake. "Gergesa" does appear in some Greek manuscripts for our account. However, the manuscripts in question antedate Origen and may reflect the influence of the church father's ingenuity, rather than witness to an early textual tradition.

While the textual witnesses to Gergesa antedate Origen, the tradition is undoubtedly pre-Origenian. Those who transcribed our manuscripts of the Gospels may have been familiar with Origen's writings, but that does not preclude the existence of Gergesa in the New Testament period, nor does it exclude the environs of the village from being a candidate for the destination of Jesus and his disciples.

Origen's description of Gergesa as an "ancient city" likely suggests that by his day, the village was in ruins. It also points to local traditions that are heard in Jewish and Christian sources. A century after Origen, Eusebius identified the location of "the border of Geshur" (Josh 13:11; Deut 3:14) north and east of the Sea of Galilee with Girgash beyond the Jordan, reflecting the Septuagintal reading (LXX Deut 3:14). He also mentions Gadara and Gerasa.

> Girgash. A city beyond the Jordan located near Gilead (Josh 13:11), which the tribe of Manasseh took (Deut 3:14). This is said to be Gerasa, the famous *polis* in Arabia. Some say it is Gadara. The Gospel also mentions the (land of) Gerasenes. (Eus. *Onom.* 64:1)

Yet, in a subsequent entry Eusebius once again demonstrates his familiarity with the village of Gergesa and local traditions connected to it.

> Gergesa. There the Lord healed the demoniacs. A village is now shown on the hill next to the Lake of Tiberias into which also the swine were cast down. (Eus. *Onom.* 74:13)

The church father's pre-Byzantine testimony to a village on the eastern shores of the Sea of Galilee is not a Christian invention. An early Jewish *midrash* makes a similar identification of Girgash [or Gergeshta] on the eastern shores of the lake.

> R. Nehemiah said: "When the Holy One, blessed is he, shows Israel the graves of Gog and Magog, the feet of the Shechinah will be on the Mount of Olives and the graves of Gog and Magog will be open from south of the Kidron Valley to *Gergeshta on the eastern side of Lake Tiberias*. (*Shir ha-Shirim Zuta* 1.4 [p. 11])

For the purposes of our study, what is important is the familiarity of both Eusebius and the Jewish *midrash* with the location of Girgash/Gergeshta/Gergesa on the eastern side of the Sea of Galilee. These local traditons were important, because Origen's description of Gergesa as an "ancient city" may indicate that by his own day the village already lay in ruins. Nevertheless, later Christian tradition strengthened the identification of Gergesa (el-Kursi), and a church was built to commemorate the Gospel event.

There is little question that on the basis of topography, the region surrounding the ancient vil-

The colonnaded street at Beth-shean (Scythopolis), with Tel Beth-shean in background. (photo S. Magal)

lage of Gergesa (el-Kursi) better suits the details presented by the Evangelists. Its location fits Matthew and Mark's description of Jesus' destination "on the other side" and Luke's "opposite Galilee." The village does not possess the problems of distance from the northern portions of the Sea of Galilee inherent in the location of Gadara, or even more acutely with Gerasa. Moreover, only in the vicinity of Gergesa do the slopes of the heights descend steeply to the shores of the Sea of Galilee. Evidence for the village's existence in antiquity is heard in rabbinical literature and the pre-Byzantine Christian writings of Origen and Eusebius. Both of the Christian writers also attest to local pre-Byzantine Christian traditions that identified Gergesa with the Gospel event.

Gergesa's only obstacle is its non-appearance in pre-Origenian manuscripts of the Gospel account. Yet the dilemma of Gergesa belongs to a well-known pattern: in the copying of ancient texts, an unknown name will almost always be "corrected" to a known name. So, it seems that in spite of its location as the place of Jesus' encounter with the demoniac, at a very early stage the name of the lesser-known village of Gergesa was exchanged for one of the two renowned cities of the Decapolis: Gadara and Gergesa.

The Decapolis. The toponym, Sea of Galilee, is the product of a creative Christian interpretation of Isaiah, "but in the latter time he will make glorious the way of the sea, the land beyond the Jordan, Galilee of the nations" (Isa 9:1b [HMT 8:23b]). Mark's use of the Christian name for the lake (Mark 1:16, 7:31) signals his embrace of this contemporary homily. It seems that the same Isaianic passage provided the narrative structure for Mark's presentation of Jesus' northern journey: "Then [Jesus] returned from the region of Tyre, and went through Sidon to the Sea of Galilee, through the region of the Decapolis" (Mark 7:31).

According to Mark, Jesus returned from Phoenicia on Isaiah's way of the sea—the trunk road from Tyre to the region of Caesarea Philippi—and then continued to the Transjordanian heights of the Hauran, which Mark identified with the region of the Decapolis. Jesus' circuitous journey concluded on the shores of the Sea of Galilee. There is little geographical logic in a route from Phoenicia to the Sea of Galilee through the Hauran. However, Mark's presentation uncannily follows the order of the topographical points in Isaiah's passage: the way of the sea, the land beyond the Jordan, Galilee of the nations. So, it seems that once again we witness Mark writing in his distinctive paraphrastic style to present Jesus' fulfillment of Isaiah's ancient prophecy.

The first historical witness to the place name Decapolis is Mark and Matthew's Gospels (Mark 5:20, 7:31; Matt 4:25). The history of this toponym has been the subject of renewed discussion. Josephus mentions "the Decapolis of Syria" in connection with a complaint brought to Vespasian by these cities against Jewish insurgents (Life 341, 410). He also describes Scythopolis as the largest city in the Decapolis (J.W. 3:446). However, the historian does not provide any additional information about the nature of the designation (geographical or political), its origins or which cities were included.

Pliny (A.D. 79) provides the most detailed first-century description of the Decapolis.

Adjoining Judaea on the side of Syria is the region of the Decapolis, so called from the number of its towns, though not all writers keep to the same list; most, however, include Damascus, with its fertile water-meadows that drain the river Chrysorrhoe, Philadelphia, Raphana (all these three withdrawn towards Arabia), Scythopolis (formerly Nysa, after Father Liber's nurse, whom he buried there), Gadara, past which flows the river Yarmuk;

THE CITIES OF THE DECAPOLIS

Hippus mentioned already, Dion, Pella rich with its waters, Galasa [i.e., Gerasa], Canatha.

(Pliny *Nat. Hist.* 5.16)

Pliny is the only writer to list *ten cities* included in the Decapolis. However, as he indicates, this list is not certain, and he acknowledges that there is disagreement among writers. His statement suggests that he is not writing from personal knowledge of the Decapolis. Instead, he is relying upon the conflicting reports of others.

The disagreement among historical witnesses is heard again in Ptolemy's *Geography*. Writing in the second century (c. A.D. 150), Ptolemy includes eighteen cities in the Decapolis. His list contains nine of Pliny's cities (omitting Raphana) and adds nine more: Heliopolis, Abila, Saana, Hina, Abila Lysanias, Capitolias, Edrei, Gadora, and Samulis (cf. Strabo *Geog.* 5.14–22). Yet what is most remarkable is that we have no mention of the Decapolis by the first-century geographer, Strabo.

Strabo describes both Syria and Palestine at some length, and even names several of the Decapolis cities: Damascus, Gadara, Philadelphia, and Scythopolis. His silence is even more curious when we recall Strabo's interest in the Lycian League, a federation of twenty-three cities in western Asia Minor organized and supervised by the Romans.

The next significant literary witness to the Decapolis is Eusebius, who reports at the beginning of the fourth century A.D., "Decapolis. In the Gospels. This is (the region) in Perea that surrounds Hippus, Pella and Gadara" (Eus. *Onom.* 80:16). Eusebius does not define the nature of the Decapolis. However, his description that it "surrounds" three cities suggests that Eusebius understood it to designate a geographical region, rather than a mere political league. Jerome's Latin translation of the *Onomasticon* specifies what may be implied in Eusebius' Greek, *regio decem urbium* (a region of ten cities). Jerome's use of *regio* to define the Decapolis echoes the earlier terminology by which Pliny described the Decapolis.

Nothing in the historical descriptions speaks of a political confederation. The only joint political effort in the Jewish Revolt is the complaint to Vespasian. These cities are not even mentioned to have sent soldiers to assist the Romans in the Jewish Revolt. Yet, modern scholarship has generally suggested that Pompey founded the league of cities when he liberated the region from Hasmonean domination in 63 B.C. While a number of the cities adopted Pompeiian eras, others did not. For example, Damascus retained its Alexandrian era.

Of greater significance, no mention is made of the Decapolis on coins for these cities, or in any first-century inscriptions yet discovered. One would have thought that with the political upheaval in the region during the first century, these cities would have proudly publicized their allegiance to the Roman Empire with mention of their membership in a political league founded by the great Roman general, Pompey. Further questions are raised about the early existence of a Roman league of cities by Augustus' assignment of Hippus and Gadara to Herod in 30 B.C. (*Ant.* 15:217; *J.W.* 1:396). It is unlikely that the emperor would have transferred these cities to a Jewish king, if they belonged to a Roman league.

It may be of some significance that apart from the references in Mark and Matthew, all of our historical references to the Decapolis occur in writings after the Jewish Revolt of A.D. 66–70. In the complete absence of any historical or epigraphical evidence to the contrary, it seems that Mark and Matthew's Decapolis—similar to the Fourth Gospel's "Bethsaida in Galilee" (John 12:21)—is an anachronistic toponym. The tumultuous events surrounding the Jewish Revolt brought significant geopolitical changes to the region. These are reflected in changing, evolving regional toponyms.

We simply do not know what the genesis was for the origins of the Decapolis. It may have stemmed from the desire of these cities to define themselves in contradistinction to the neighboring regions heavily populated with Jews, who had recently rebelled against Rome. Use of the term

The Roman theater at Scythopolis (Beth-shean). (photo S. Magal)

The spring area at Hammath Gader, generally identified with Gadara of the Decapolis. (NEAEHL)

in the Gospels may reflect the period in which the individual writings were composed (i.e., post–A.D. 70), because there is no corroborating evidence to suggest that the Decapolis was known in the days of Jesus. Those familiar with the history of the Land of Israel in an earlier age will recognize the same phenomenon in the Hebrew Scriptures' use of an anachronistic toponym to designate the coastal plain as "the land of the Philistines" (Gen 21:32) in the time of Abraham—centuries before the actual arrival of the Philistines. In both instances, they tell us more about the toponymic usage at the time of the composition than place names in the period described.

CHAPTER 6

THE LAST DAYS OF JESUS

𝔄LL OF THE GOSPELS agree that the Romans crucified Jesus outside of Jerusalem. Roman responsibility for the death of Jesus is also recounted in one of the earliest Christian baptismal creeds: "[he] suffered under [the Roman prefect] Pontius Pilate." Yet, the topographical and historical details surrounding Jesus' execution vary in the reports of the New Testament. It is not possible to engage here the complex issues of the literary relationship of the four Gospels as historical sources for the Passion narratives. Much is written about the subject elsewhere. Our interest is more narrowly focused to determine what can be known of the physical setting of Jerusalem, and what that setting can inform us about the historical events that unfolded on it.

One hundred years of archaeological activity in Jerusalem, begun at the end of the nineteenth century, have helped to illuminate the physical setting of Jerusalem during the New Testament period. Questions still remain, but new data have provided fresh insights. The results have sometimes challenged long-held traditions attached to sacred sites. Nevertheless, a clearer picture has emerged about those fateful days. We shall attempt to sketch the historical framework for the events of that week, with particular attention given to their topographical setting.

Jesus approached Jerusalem in the days leading up to Passover (John 11:55). His pilgrimage continued a family practice. During the days of the Second Temple, it was not a necessary requirement to travel to Jerusalem three times a year as obligated at Sinai: "Three times in the year shall all your males appear before the Lord God" (Exod 23:17; cf. 30:23). The impracticality of traveling long distances thrice yearly—particularly difficult from the remoteness of the Jewish dispersion—necessitated a figurative interpretation of the injunction, "to appear before the Lord" (Tob 1:6–10; *Midr. Tanh.* [Buber ed.] *Tezawe* (51b); *Ant.* 4:203–204).

Nevertheless, Luke records the piety of Jesus' family—"Now his parents went to Jerusalem every year at the feast of the Passover" (Luke 2:41). Jesus' familiarity with the setting of Jerusalem indicates he was accustomed to—and perhaps a familiar figure in—the city at the time of Passover, "The Teacher says, 'Where is my guest room, where I am to eat the Passover with my disciples?'" (Mark 14:14; Luke 22:7–13).

The northern ford across the Jordan River, which would have been used by a pilgrim who desired to travel to Jerusalem through Perea in the Transjordan, lay within the territory of Scythopolis (cf. *Ant.* 12:348). This independent Greek city was situated between the geopolitical regions of Galilee and Samaria. The city and its territory belonged to the province of Syria and were not part of the lands granted to Herod's sons upon his death. As a statement of the geographical and political realities that existed in the days of Jesus, Luke's description that Jesus "passed between Samaria and Galilee" in Luke 17:11 is correct and can hardly be deemed, as is sometimes charged to be, evidence of Luke's "geographical ineptitude."

According to the Gospels, Jesus did not always use the same route in his pilgrimage to Jerusalem. Testimony on an earlier occasion (John 4:4–6) of Jesus' presence in the interior of Samaria suggests that at times he followed the watershed route through the central hill country. This route was the most direct, taking only three days from Galilee to Jerusalem (*Life* 268–270). Yet, because of violence between the Jews and Samaritans, it was often considered too dangerous (*J.W.* 2:232–233; *Ant.* 20:118; Luke 10:30–37). A third route from Galilee mentioned in the ancient sources led along the foothills of Mount Ephraim to Antipatris and ascended the Beth-horon ridge to Jerusalem (*J.W.* 2:228). However, we have no mention of this route in connection with Jesus' pilgrimages to the Holy City.

Mention of his travel through Jericho (Matt 20:29; Mark 10:46; Luke 19:1) indicates that Jesus' pilgrimage from Galilee led him through the region of the Transjordan and along the Roman road from Jericho (cf. Luke 10:30) that followed near the biblical Ascent of Adummim (Josh 15:7). That route would have taken him within sight of the former Hasmonean and Herodian palaces at Jericho. Indeed, it seems that the physical presence of the former residence of Archelaus, son of Herod, may

JESUS' LAST JOURNEY TO JERUSALEM

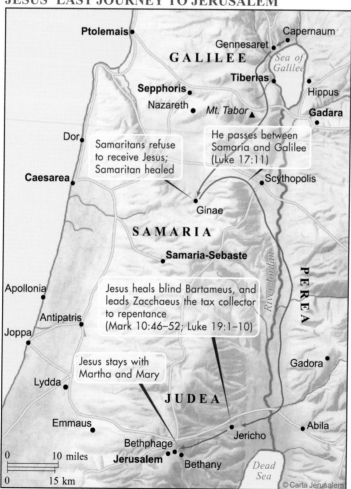

have been the cue for Jesus to adopt the well-known story of "the Herodian son who would be king" (*Ant.* 17:342–343; *J.W.* 2:111–113; Dio Cass. 55.27.6; Strabo *Geog.* 2.46) as the inspiration for his parable: "A man of noble birth went into a far country to receive a kingdom and then return" (Luke 19:12).

Only Luke relates that Jesus told the parable as they passed out of Jericho, and likewise only in the Third Gospel does Jesus use the story of the Herodian scion as the narrative kernel for his parabolic creativity. The collocation of the parable with strong historical allusions to the son of Herod and the magnificently restored residence that symbolized the royalty he sought but never attained, is remarkable. Recent excavations have determined that an earthquake destroyed the palaces in A.D. 48, and they were abandoned long before scholarship assumes that Luke wrote his Gospel. It seems the source for Luke's unique combination of the parable and the physical setting of the environs of Jericho must have originated from a time when the palace still stood, or at least its memory was still fresh.

As Jesus approached Jerusalem he reached the eastern slopes of the Mount of Olives. On the outskirts of Jerusalem lay the villages of Bethany (Neh 11:32; Eus. *Onom.* 58:15) and Bethphage (Luke 19:29). The latter was positioned between Bethany and Jerusalem and marked the outer limits of the Holy City (*m. Men.* 11:2; *b. Pesah.* 63b). Its name was derived from the Semitic word for unripened figs (see Eus. *Onom.* 58:13) and may indicate agricultural activity in the vicinity (Mark 11:20). In the same vein, the toponym "Mount of Olives" (Zech 14:4) was also de-

JERICHO AREA TODAY

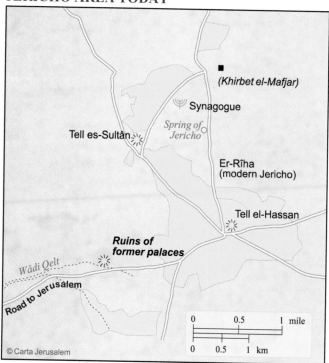

PLAN OF ROMAN JERICHO

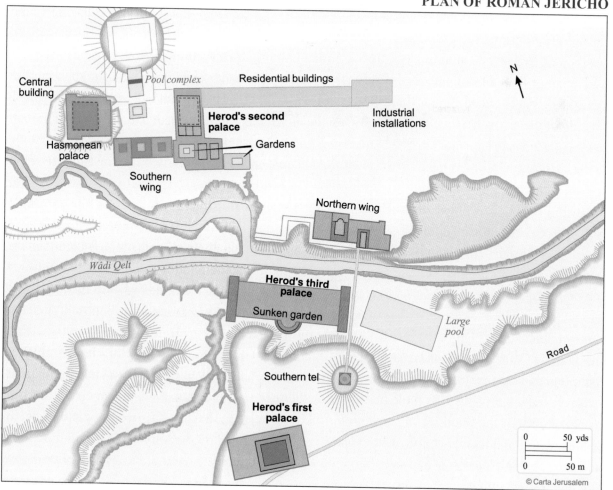

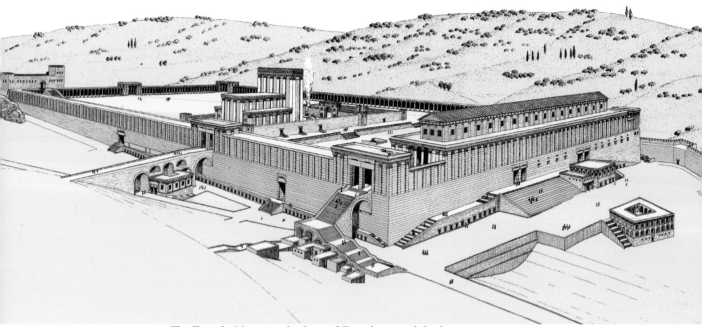

The Temple Mount in the Second Temple period, looking east. (reconstruction L. Ritemeyer)

termined from local produce.

The New Testament records that Jesus stayed in Bethany (Matt 21:17; Mark 11:11), perhaps in the home of Lazarus, Mary and Martha (Luke 10:38; John 11:1). The large influx of visitors (cf. *Ant.* 18:313) during the pilgrimage feasts meant that many pilgrims had to stay outside of the Holy City (*Ant.* 17:213–214). Bethany is situated less than 2 miles (3 km) from Jerusalem (John 11:18), making it a convenient place for daily access to Jerusalem and the Temple. The Gospels portray Jesus' trips back and forth between Bethany and Jerusalem (Mark 11:11–12). However, even pilgrims who stayed outside of the city were required to eat within the city walls the offering sacrificed on the Passover eve—14/15 Nisan (*m. Pesah.* 7:9, 7:12, 10:3). The disciples' efforts to arrange the meal within the city walls of Jerusalem (Luke 22:7–13) are one of the clearest indications that for the Last Supper Jesus followed the rabbinic stipulations regarding the Passover meal.

During the week leading up to Passover, Jesus was teaching daily in the Temple (Luke 19:47). Study of the Scripture within the temple precincts is recorded in Jewish tradition (*m. Tamid* 5:1; *m. Yoma* 1:7). It was also a place of study familiar to Jesus from his youth (Luke 2:48–49). The colonnaded porticoes surrounding the Temple likely included these places of study (cf. Acts 5:12). In addition, the platform atop the steps of ascent leading from the south into the Huldah Gates of the Temple Mount was a place where teaching was reported (*t. Sanh.* 2:2; *m. Sanh.* 11:2). The Mishnah describes three courts of law, "One used to sit at the gate of the Temple Mount, one used to sit at the gate of the Temple Court, and one used to sit in the Chamber of Hewn Stone" (*Sanh.* 11:2). The first of these locations may be identified near the broad platform atop the steps to the Huldah Gates.

It is in the vicinity of the Temple that Jesus challenged financial transactions that came under the responsibility of the Sadducean priesthood (Luke 19:45–46). Scholarship has tried to identify Jesus' actions within the temple courts. The expanded narrative of Mark does imply Jesus' actions were within the temple precincts and even directed against the Temple itself, "and he would not allow any one to carry anything through the temple" (Mark 11:16; cf. John 2:15). On the other hand, Matthew and Luke omit Mark's portrayal that Jesus' actions were aimed at the institution of the Temple, but instead at the priests entrusted with its care. Moreover, Luke's verbal description does not necessarily indicate Jesus' presence already within the temple precincts.

Luke's account is supported by the Jewish sources. The mishnaic tractate *Berakhot* 9:5 states that one was not even permitted to ascend to the Temple Mount with a purse, let alone that it was the site of a marketplace: "He may not enter into the Temple Mount with his staff or his sandal or his purse." It seems likely that Jesus' actions took place either in the area of shops, recently excavated adjacent to the southern and southwestern walls of the Temple Mount, or the enclosed Royal Stoa (*Ant.* 15:411–416) in the southern portion of the Temple Mount. In an apocryphal story of the life of Jesus, we find him mentioned among the ritual baths near the shops south of the Temple Mount: "And [Jesus] took them and brought them into the place of purification itself and walked about in the temple" (P. Oxy 840; cf. John 11:55; Acts 21:24, 26).

The cause for Jesus' protest is not explicitly stated. A recent study of this episode in light of contemporary Jewish sources suggests that Jesus—like others of his contemporaries—objected to the House of Annas' evasion of personal tithes to the Lord and oppressive measures. Jesus was certainly not alone in his assessment that this priestly clan (Luke 3:2; John 18:13; Acts 4:6) had misused its position as stewards of the temple finances.

> The Sages said: The (produce) stores for the children of Hanin [=Annas] were destroyed three years before the rest of the Land of Israel, because they failed to set aside tithes from their produce, for they interpreted *Thou shalt surely tithe…and thou shalt surely eat* as excluding the seller, and *The increase of thy seed* as excluding the buyer. (*Sifre*; cf. *y. Pe'ah* 1:6)

The southern steps leading to the Temple Mount, Jerusalem. (photo S. Magal)

The Temple Mount today with the Dome of the Rock at its center, looking east toward the Mount of Olives.
(photo S. Magal)

The description of the House of Annas being both "sellers" and "buyers" in *Sifre* may help to explain Matthew and Mark's expanded description of the targets of Jesus' rebuke. The Evangelists' combination of sellers and buyers is a derivation from an earlier hendiadys. While Luke states that Jesus expelled only "the sellers" (cf. John 2:14), the other two Evangelists speak of "those who sold and those who bought." The rabbinic witness suggests that in all of the Gospels Jesus is only concerned with the abuses of the temple hierocracy (see also *Tg. Isa.* 5:7–10; *b. B. Bat.* 3b–4a; *Ant.* 15:260–262, 20:181, 20:205–207).

Jesus' words and actions in the days leading up to Passover were interpreted as a challenge to the Sadducean temple establishment. Yet, his message shared a broad public appeal, and they could not arrest him openly (Luke 19:48). He gave voice to popular discontent (Luke 20:19), and a response by the temple establishment had to wait until a more opportune moment.

On the eve of Passover, preparations were made for the festive meal. While the priests offered other sacrificial offerings, Scripture stipulated that the people themselves were to sacrifice this offering in the Temple (Deut 16:2; *m. Pesah.* 5:6; Philo *Spec.* 2.145). The sacrifice could only be performed on the 14th of Nisan, and it was to be eaten that evening (Deut 16:6). The Gospels are silent on the details of preparation leading up to the meal, likely because they were so commonplace as to need no report.

CHAPTER 7

JESUS AND THE MYTH OF AN ESSENE QUARTER IN JERUSALEM

SIXTY YEARS OF SCHOLARSHIP CONCERNING THE DEAD SEA SCROLLS have brought clearer understanding concerning a fascinating stream of Jewish piety that existed during the final days of the Second Temple. These writings belong to the interwoven fabric of thought that is so important as a background to our reading of the New Testament. Some scholars have attempted to discern whether there existed direct contact between the Qumran Congregation and figures in the New Testament. In particular, similarities between John the Baptist and the Qumran Congregation regarding their baptisms, their self-identification with Isaiah 40:3 (see Matt 3:3; Mark 1:3; Luke 3:4; John 1: 23; 1QS 8:13-34) and their apocalyptic rhetoric, have drawn some to conclude that John may have at one time had direct contact with the Essenes.

While similarities between the Qumran writings and the Baptist do exist, the parallels with Jesus are by contrast lacking. Nevertheless, there are still those who seek to establish a direct link between Jesus and the Essenes. One of the more popular notions is that Jesus abandoned the appointed day for Passover in the Temple and embraced the Essene solar calendar to observe the feast two days early. In the 1950s Annie Jaubert first suggested this novel idea in an attempt to reconcile the chronologies of the Synoptic Gospels and John. The former presents Jesus' death on the first day of Passover, while John implies that the Jewish feast had not yet begun (John 19:14). Instead, according to the Fourth Gospel, Jesus' death coincided with the sacrifice of the Passover lamb on the eve of the holiday (cf. John 19:35; LXX Exod 12:46).

Those familiar with the complex literary relationships between the Gospels recognize that Jaubert's solution does not really resolve the differences but merely jettisons the historical framework of the Synoptic Gospels in lieu of John's creative theological presentation of Christ as the paschal lamb (cf. 1 Cor 5:7; *Mek. on Exod* 12:3; Horowitz and Rabin ed. 1970:24–25). Nonetheless, others have built upon Jaubert's thesis to advance the notion that Jesus ate the Last Supper in a first-century Essene Quarter on today's Mount Zion.

The Myth of the Essene Quarter. Quite simply, there exists today not a single piece of *archaeological* evidence to demonstrate that an Essene Quarter existed in Jerusalem in Jesus' day. Much of the conjecture stems from F. J. Bliss's discovery of a gate on the southern edge of the western hill. The Roman period gate may be the one mentioned by Josephus.

> Beginning at the same point [i.e., Hippicus Tower] in the other direction, westward, [the wall] descended past the place called Bethso to the Gate of the Essenes, then turned southwards above the fountain of Siloam; thence it again inclined to the east towards Solomon's pool, and after passing a spot which they call Ophlas [i.e., the Ophel], finally joined the eastern portico of the temple. (*J.W.* 5:145)

Notwithstanding Bliss's identification of the Essene Gate, there is nothing to suggest that this gate was named after an Essene Quarter inside of the city. Instead, the gates of Jerusalem are often named for points of destination outside of the city. The Hebrew names for today's Jaffa Gate and Damascus Gate are modern examples of this phenomenon. Likewise in antiquity, the eastern gate of Jerusalem exiting the precincts of the Temple was identified by its direction towards Susa, the capital of Persia (*m. Mid.* 1:3; cf. *m. Kel.* 17:9). Finally, Josephus reports that the only gate in the northern section of the First Wall was called the Gennath (Garden) Gate (*J.W.* 5:146), apparently because it led to the outskirts of the city, where there were orchards and gardens.

If we follow the nomenclature of these other first-century gates, it seems more likely that the term "Gate of the Essenes" indicated that the gate faced an Essene settlement outside of Jerusalem. Qumran-style shaft tombs recently discovered at Beit Safafa south of Jerusalem may have belonged to the kind of settlement towards which the Gate of the Essenes was oriented. Unfortunately, we do not have more information about the community that used these tombs. In the same way, we have no information how the Gate of the Essenes acquired its name. Lacking further evidence, there is no compelling reason to assume that the Gate of the Essenes signified an Essene Quarter within the walled city of Jerusalem.

Remains of the Essene community at Qumran, looking west. (photo A. Alon)

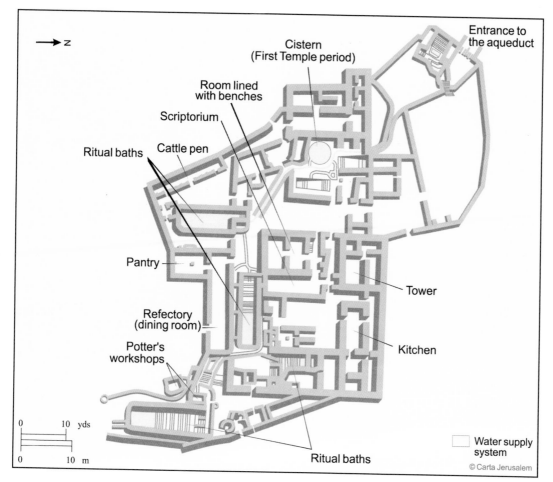

Entrance to the aqueduct

Cistern (First Temple period)

Room lined with benches

Scriptorium

Ritual baths · Cattle pen

Pantry

Refectory (dining room)

Potter's workshops

Tower

Kitchen

Ritual baths

Water supply system

© Carta Jerusalem

0 10 yds

0 10 m

Apart from the Gate of the Essenes, the only material evidence offered to suggest an Essene Quarter are the ritual baths (*miqva'ot*) discovered in the vicinity of the gate. Some scholars have ascribed particular significance to the parapet dividing the stairs leading into the baths. While the ritual baths at Qumran do have this feature, it is a mistake to conclude that the parapet and *miqva'ot* on Mount Zion indicate that they belonged to an Essene community. The parapet was not a unique Essene feature, but a common characteristic in ritual baths to prevent physical contact between the ritually defiled person entering the mikveh and the ritually purified individual leaving the mikveh (cf. *m. Mid.* 2:2; Let. Aris. 160).

Immersion baths with a parapet were not limited to Qumran and Mount Zion. They can still be seen among the numerous *miqva'ot* below the southern wall of the Temple Mount. These were intended for Jewish pilgrims to purify themselves before entering the temple precincts (e.g., Acts 21:26; P. Oxy 840). By contrast, the Qumran Congregation considered the current priestly leadership of the Temple illegitimate and their service in the Temple defiled (cf. CD 6:11–13; 4:15–18; 5:6–7). According to Josephus, the Essenes had ceased active participation in the temple service (*Ant.* 18:19). It would have been highly improbable to find first-century Essene ritual baths in Jerusalem intended for purification and participation in the temple services.

A final instance of archaeological evidence actually indicates that the *miqva'ot* in the vicinity of the Gate of the Essenes did *not* belong to an Essene Quarter. Some of the stepped *miqva'ot* also have an adjoining collection pool. The small adjoining pool (*otzar*) is a Pharisaic custom (*m. Miqw.*

The Qumran caves where the Dead Sea Scrolls were discovered. (photo Mike Horton)

6:8). Other pious groups adopted the Pharisaic practice but not Qumranians. In other words, while we cannot be certain who used the ritual baths on Mount Zion, on the basis of the archaeological evidence at Qumran we can exclude those who followed the ritual practices of the Qumran Congregation.

Josephus' reference to Bethso in the passage where he mentions the Gate of the Essenes has been associated by some to the instructions for the Congregation living in eschatological Jerusalem.

> You are to build them a precinct for latrines outside the city. They shall go out there, on the northwest of the city: roofed outhouses with pits inside, into which the excrement will descend so as not to be visible. The outhouses must be three thousand cubits from any part of the city. (11QTemple 46:13–16)

It is interesting that the direction of the latrines in the Temple Scroll northwest of the eschatological city is in the general direction of Josephus' Bethso near the Hippicus Tower. Even before the discovery of the Dead Sea Scrolls, Josephus' enigmatic term was thought to represent the Hebrew *beit tzo'ah* (latrine). Nevertheless, the portrayal of latrines northwest of eschatological Jerusalem—even if this is the meaning for Bethso near Hippicus Tower—is not evidence for an Essene Quarter on Mount Zion. The description of the Essene latrines in the Temple Scroll is not near Mount Zion, and Josephus makes no mention that Bethso possessed any special connection with the Essenes. In the end, we are left with disparate passages whose relationship is in question and that individually provide little tangible evidence for an Essene presence in first-century Jerusalem.

Jesus and the Essene Passover. Is there internal evidence within the Gospel narratives that can assist us to discern whether Jesus adopted the Essene preference of the solar calendar over the lunar calendar used in the Temple? Did he likewise share their estimation that the first-century

Temple was defiled? Obviously, Jesus' pilgrimage to Jerusalem at Passover makes no sense, if he shared the Essene rejection of the current Temple. Celebration of Passover was permitted for Jews outside of Jerusalem. Pilgrimage to the Holy City at the time of the biblical feast served only to make possible participation in the Temple and to observe the Passover meal within the city walls.

During the week before Passover, Jesus stayed in Bethany (Mark 11:11). As the feast approached he arranged for a room within the walls of the city to celebrate the Passover meal. The setting for the Last Supper within the walled city of Jerusalem is one of the most compelling arguments that the Last Supper was indeed a Passover meal. According to rabbinical prescriptions, it was required that those who shared in the lamb sacrificed in the Temple on the eve of Passover (the 14th of Nisan) ate it that very evening (Ex 12:10; m. *Zebah.* 5:8; m. *Pesah.* 10:9; cf. m. *Ber.* 1:1) and within the walls of Jerusalem (m. *Pesah.* 7:9, 12; 10:3).

The provision to eat the Passover lamb within the city walls was a practical accommodation to the spatial limits of the temple precincts. The sheer number of pilgrims did not allow the continuation of the earlier requirement to eat the meal within the precincts of the Temple. The relaxing of this limitation by Israel's Sages is not the opinion shared by the Book of Jubilees, a work that belonged to the Qumran library:

> And in the days when the house has been built in the name of the Lord in the land of their inheritance, they shall go there and slay the passover in the evening, at sunset, at the third part of the day. And they shall offer its blood on the threshold of the altar, and shall place its fat on the fire that is upon the altar, and *they shall eat its flesh roasted with fire in the court of the house that has been sanctified in the name of the Lord.* (Jub 49:19–20)

We have noted that the Essenes withdrew from participation in the temple sacrifices. According to Jubilees, however, even if they had participated in the Passover sacrifice in the Temple they would have eaten the festive meal within the temple precincts and not on Mount Zion.

What is unrecorded but presumed—because it was so commonplace as not to be considered worthy of mention by the New Testament writers—is the fact that shortly before the Passover meal, Jesus and those who accompanied him from Galilee ascended to the Temple and sacrificed the paschal lamb. This was the only offering that was sacrificed by the people themselves and not the priests. Groups of pilgrims and inhabitants from Jerusalem would join to slaughter the paschal lamb. There were some who were of the opinion that the lamb could not be sacrificed by an individual but required the quorum of ten men. In any event, it seems that those who gathered in the Temple on the eve of Passover formed groups to complete the sacrifice (cf. m. *Pesah.* 8:7; *Tg. Ps.-J.* on Exod 12:4; *J.W.* 6:423–433; t. *Pesah.* 4:3). While a portion of the victim would have been left for the sacrifice (Lev 3:3–4; m. *Pesah.* 5:10) most of the lamb was taken by the people and served at the festive meal.

Indication that the paschal lamb was part of the Last Supper is attested in the words of Jesus, "I have earnestly desired to eat this *paschal lamb* (or *Passover*) with you…" (Luke 22:15). Christian readers seldom recognize the idiomatic Hebraism in Luke's Greek. The name for the holiday (Passover) is likewise the same Greek or Hebrew term for the sacrificial offering served at the meal (i.e., the lamb). So, translators render the Greek word in the Apostle Paul's declaration, "For Christ, our *Passover lamb* has been sacrificed" (1 Cor 5:7).

If the Passover lamb was a part of the Last Supper, then it is impossible that the meal coincided with the Essene Passover. The paschal lamb could be sacrificed *only* in the Temple and *only* on the 14th of Nisan in accordance with the lunar calendar adopted by the Temple (Exod 12:6; m. *Pesah.* 5:3,

5). The Essene Passover meal occurred that year two days earlier. The very fact that a sacrificial lamb was included in the meal of Jesus, excludes his participation with the Essenes at Passover. The Qumran writings and the testimony of Josephus both indicate that the Essenes, because of their rejection of the current Temple, had abandoned active participation in the temple sacrifices— including the Passover. In other words, unlike the Passover celebrated by Jesus, there would have been no Passover lamb at the Tuesday-evening Passover of the Essenes.

Two additional details from the New Testament account of the Last Supper strengthen our reading that the Passover of Jesus was not an Essene meal. Jesus and those who celebrated the biblical feast with him are portrayed *reclining at the table* (Matt 26:20; Mark 14:18). Even the Gospel of John, whose Passion chronology is assumed to suggest that the Last Supper coincided with the Essene Passover, describes Jesus and those at the table *reclining* (John 13:23, 28; cf. 12:2). This description, of course, reflects the Jewish practice to recline at the Passover. According to Josephus, however, the Essene custom was to dine while *sitting* (*J.W.* 2:130). The archaeologists found no benches that would have been used for dining couches at Khirbet Qumran. This appears to agree with Josephus' testimony that the Essenes did not recline but sat at their meals. It further suggests that Jesus did not follow the Essene custom of sitting at the meal for the Last Supper.

Finally, the dishes discovered at Khirbet Qumran indicate another variation between the custom of the Qumran Congregation and Jesus at the Last Supper. As archaeologist Jodi Magness observed, in ancient Judaea typically light meals consisted of bread dipped in a wine-based vinegar. Main meals were a lentil or vegetable stew served in a large common bowl that was sopped up with bread. Josephus' description of the Essene meals and the numerous individual bowls, cups

The Cenaculum, traditional site of the Last Supper, located on today's Mount Zion. (photo D. Bahat)

"And he took a cup, and when he had given thanks he said, 'Take this, and divide it among yourselves'" (Luke 22:17), *engraving by William James Linton (1812–1897) from a 19th century Bible.* (Carta collection)

and plates at Qumran suggest they did not follow the normal custom of eating from a common dish. The practice was likely a consequence of their stringent concerns regarding ritual impurity that could be transmitted through food and drink. As such, the large number of dishes found at Qumran is consistent with Josephus' description of their meals: "The cook sets before each *one plate* with a single course" (*J.W.* 2:130).

Yet, the Essene practice was not the custom of Jesus at the Last Supper. He used the act of dipping in a common dish to identify his betrayer. "He who has dipped his hand in the dish with me, will betray me" (Matt 26:23; Mark 14:20; cf. John 13:26). Likewise, the Gospels attest to a common cup for the *Qiddush*. "And he took a cup, and when he had given thanks he said, "Take this, and divide among yourselves'" (Luke 22:17). Jesus' actions would not have been permitted in an Essene setting.

While Jesus shared the Pharisaic critique of the first-century Sadducean priestly dynasty—the House of Hanin (Luke 3:2; Acts 4:6; *b. Pesah.* 57a; *t. Menah.* 13:21)—he gives no hint that he shared the Essene rejection of the sanctity of the temple service. Jesus' followers continued to frequent the Temple, even after the Cross (Luke 24:53; Acts 2:46). The vicinity of the Temple is also likely the setting for the outpouring of the Holy Spirit on the Jewish feast of Pentecost. Even the Apostle Paul had no qualms about submitting to ritual immersion and ascending to the Temple to offer sacrifices (Acts 21:17–26). These are hardly actions by a movement that saw the Temple as spiritually irrelevant. Consequently, the picture presented by modern archaeology and the New Testament is consistent. There is nothing in the material or historical record to suggest that Jesus abandoned the Jerusalem Temple or shared his final Passover meal in an Essene Quarter on Mount Zion.

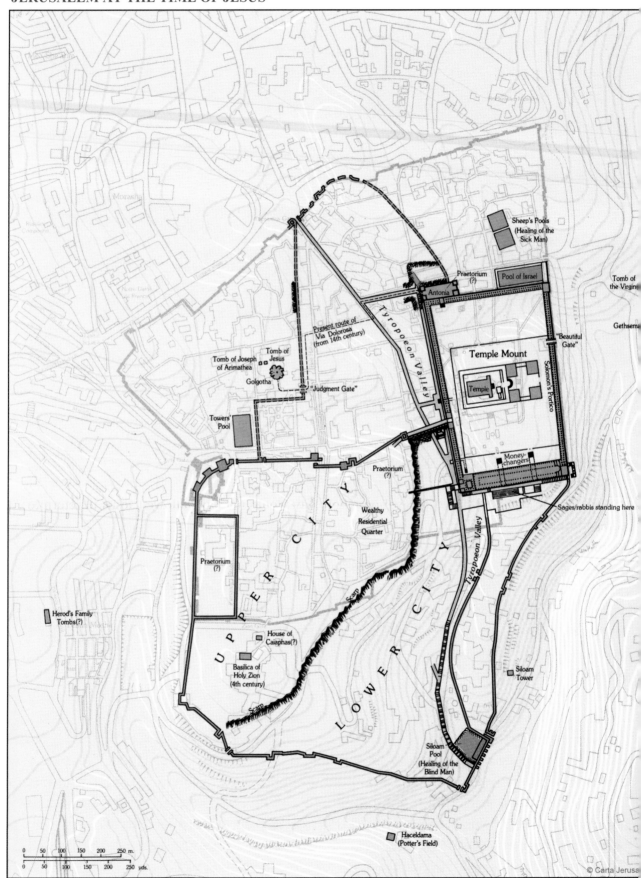

Sheep's Pools
(Healing of the
Sick Man)

Praetorium
(?)

Pool of Israel

Tomb of
the Virgin

Antonia

Gethsema

Present route of
Via Dolorosa
(from 14th century)

Tyropoeon Valley

"Beautiful
Gate"

Temple Mount

Tomb of Joseph
of Arimathea

Tomb of
Jesus

Temple

Solomon's Portico

Golgotha

"Judgment Gate"

Towers'
Pool

Money-
changers

U P P E R   C I T Y

Praetorium
(?)

Sages/rabbis standing here

Wealthy
Residential
Quarter

Tyropoeon Valley

Praetorium
(?)

Scarp

L O W E R   C I T Y

Herod's Family
Tombs(?)

House of
Caiaphas(?)

Siloam
Tower

Basilica of
Holy Zion
(4th century)

Scarp

Siloam
Pool
(Healing of the
Blind Man)

| 0 | 50 | 100 | 150 | 200 | 250 m. |

| 0 | 50 | 100 | 150 | 200 | 250 yds. |

Haceldama
(Potter's Field)

© Carta Jerusa

CHAPTER 8

THE ARREST AND DEATH OF JESUS

ILGRIMS TO JERUSALEM ascended to the Temple and offered the sacrificial lambs—the *Pesach* (Mark 14:12; Luke 22:15; 1 Cor 5:7)—that were then served as the main course for those celebrating Passover in the Holy City (Deut 16:5–6). We have no clear indication where Jesus shared this meal. Mark (14:15) and Luke (22:12) merely describe that it was in a "room upstairs." In the fifth century Byzantine Christian tradition began to locate this room on the southern slopes of the western hill of Jerusalem, yet corroborating literary or archaeological evidence is lacking.

What is more clear is that after the hymns of praise were sung (Matt 26:30; Mark 14:26; i.e., the *Hallel* of Ps 113–118) that conclude the Passover meal, Jesus and his disciples then retreated to the slopes of the Mount of Olives (Luke 22:39; Matt 26:30; Mark 14:26). Matthew and Mark further specify that the place was called Gethsemane (Matt 26:36; Mark 14:32)—a topographical name unknown in any other first-century source (cf. Eus. *Onom.* 74:16).

Restrictions on the distance of travel on a holy day would not have allowed Jesus to return to Bethany that evening. The celebrants were required to remain within the boundaries of the city overnight. The Mount of Olives laid within "a sabbath's day journey" (Acts 1:12)—the limits of travel to which an observant Jew was restricted on the holy day. Jesus may have been drawn to a specific site on the Mount of Olives by custom (Luke 22:39) to a focal point of prayer where tradition remembered the place of King David's prayer (*y. Ber.* 4:8b [based on 2 Sam 15:32]).

After a time of prayer, the Gospels report that one of Jesus' followers—Judas Iscariot—led a contingent of the high priests and their soldiers to arrest him. Judas' role was not to identify Jesus, who was well known to the temple establishment, but to locate Jesus' entourage and to distinguish them from others who were likely encamped on the hillside. Under the cloak of darkness, Jesus was arrested and led away to the house of the high priest, Joseph bar Caiapha (Caiaphas).

Christian tradition has located the high priest's house on the southern portions of the western hill. Nevertheless, recent excavations carried out in today's Jewish Quarter of Jerusalem uncovered an inscribed weight measure from the home of Bar Kathros, another family of high priests. This family is remembered in the Babylonian Talmud in the context of criticisms toward high priestly dynasties from the Roman period. These priests were criticized for their oppression, secrecy and financial misconduct. In a saying remembered by the second-generation *tanna*, Abba Saul b. Batnit:

Woe is me because of the house of Boethus;
    Woe is me because of their staves!
Woe is me because of the house of Hanin (=Annas);
    Woe is me because of their whisperings!
Woe is me because of the house of Kathros;
    Woe is me because of their pens!
Woe is me because of the house of Ishmael the son of Phabi;
    Woe is me because of their fists!
For they are High Priests and their sons are [temple] treasurers and their sons-in-law are trustees and their servants beat the people with staves. (*b. Pesah.* 57a=*t. Menah.* 13:21)

Stone weight from the "Burnt House" in the Jewish Quarter of Jerusalem inscribed "(belonging) to Bar Kathros."
(NEAEHL)

Three features from this talmudic witness are important for our concerns. First, the complaint against these families of treachery is coupled with mention of their control over the finances of the Temple. This corresponds to Jesus and the Sages' complaint against the House of Annas (Mark 11:17). Second, we hear a specific charge against the family of Hanin (Annas), which the Gospels describe secretly handed Jesus to the Romans. Their "whisperings" indicate "secret conclaves to devise oppressive measures" (*b. Pesah.* 57a n. b2; cf. *Ant.* 20:199, 13:294). Finally, mention of the Bar Kathros family in the inscription and the Talmud assists to identify the vicinity of a family of priests (see *Ant.* 20:16) whose home in Jerusalem was destroyed during the Roman siege in the summer of A.D. 70.

Discovery of monumental homes near the Bar Kathros house has raised the possibility that this area may have been a neighborhood of other high priestly families. One designated by the archaeologists, "the Palatial Mansion," is remarkable for its size and elegance. It was a multistoried home, over 5,500 square feet [c. 600 sq. m] in size. It contained imported vessels, and its plastered walls were covered with frescoes, newly refashioned to imitate contemporary Roman styles just prior to its destruction. A signature glass pitcher discovered within the ruins was the work of the renowned glass-maker, Ennion of Sidon. The residents of this house must have been a particularly notable and wealthy family, and the exceptional number of *miqva'ot* may indicate that they were a family of high priests.

We have no way of determining whether this home belonged to the family of Annas or Caiaphas. However, the opulence and accumulation of wealth exhibited in "the Palatial Mansion" characterize the economic position of the longest hierocratic dynasty in the first century A.D. (*Ant.* 20:198). They were the targets of harsh criticism in their day, as we have heard both from Jesus and Abba Saul b. Batnit.

At daybreak Jesus was brought to "the Sanhedrin" (Luke 22:66; cf. Matt 26:59; Mark 14:55). This is Luke's only use of the term in his Gospel. In Acts (4:15; 5:27, 34; 6:12, 15) he employs the term not to designate the council but the council-chamber, the Chamber of Hewn Stone mentioned in the Jewish sources (*m. Pe'ah* 2:6; *m. Sanh.* 11:2; *m. Mid.* 5:4; *y. Sanh.* 19c). Luke's reading of council-chamber rather than an indication of the participation of the full Sanhedrin in Jesus' condemnation and transfer to the Romans, concurs with testimony about the Sanhedrin's concern to preserve human life and strong reluctance to execute capital punishment.

A Sanhedrin that puts someone to death in a week [i.e., in seven years] is called "destructive." Rabbi Eleazar ben

Azariah says: "Even one person in seventy years." Rabbi Tarfon and Rabbi Akiva say: "If we had been members of the Sanhedrin, no one would ever have been put to death." (*m. Maksh.* 1:10)

In addition, the understanding that only the clan of Annas (i.e., Annas, Caiaphas, John and Alexander; cf. Acts 4:6) and those close to them were present in the Chamber of Hewn Stone and questioned Jesus, is more fitting with the subsequent steps taken by Jesus' accusers. Their actions would hardly have gained the required approval of the full Sanhedrin (Luke 23:50–51).

To deliver a fellow Jew into the hands of the Romans with the possibility of his execution was considered in Jewish opinion a transgression of such magnitude that it was eternally unforgivable (*S. 'Olam Rab.* ch. 3 end). With the same overriding concern for a single human life (cf. *m. Sanh.* 4:5), we hear in the Jerusalem Talmud that even if the Romans have surrounded the city:

> And they say, "Give us one from among you and we will kill him. And if you do not, we will kill all of you." Even if all of you may be killed, you shall not hand over a single soul from Israel. (*y. Ter.* 8:10)

So, we hear later of the concern by these same Sadducean priests that their clandestine actions might become public knowledge (Acts 5:28).

Finally, still another piece of evidence demonstrates that Jesus could not have been condemned to death by the Sanhedrin. According to the mishnaic tractate *Sanhedrin* there were two graves reserved for those executed by order of the supreme council.

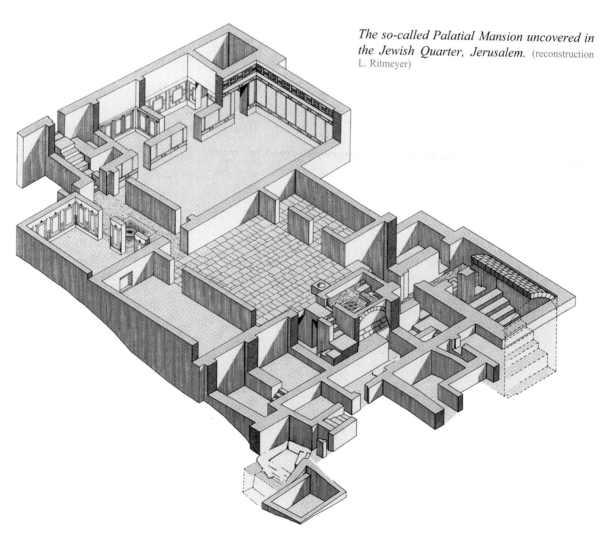

The so-called Palatial Mansion uncovered in the Jewish Quarter, Jerusalem. (reconstruction L. Ritmeyer)

Remains of Herod's palace at Caesarea. (photo S. Magal)

CAESAREA—PLAN OF THE CITY

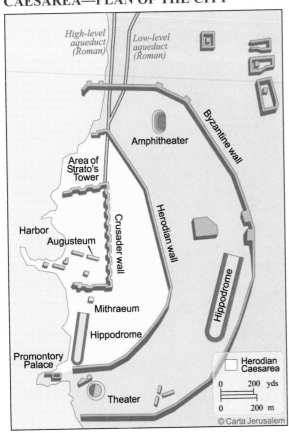

They used not to bury [the condemned man] in the burying-place of his fathers, but two burying-places were kept in readiness by the court, one for them that were beheaded or strangled, and one for them that were stoned or burnt.

(*m. Sanh.* 9:6)

The Gospel accounts are unanimous that Jesus was not laid in one of these two tombs (Matt 27:60; Mark 15:46; Luke 23:53; John 19:41).

After a period of initial inquiry, Jesus was taken to the Roman prefect, Pontius Pilate, and accused of political sedition (Luke 23:2). Normally, Pilate resided in Caesarea, the capital of the Roman province of Judea. However, to maintain a show of imperial power before the crowds gathered for Passover, the Gospels record that Pilate came to Jerusalem and resided at the Praetorium (Matt 27:27; Mark 15:16; John 18:28).

Christian tradition has identified the site of the Praetorium with the Antonia Fortress, built by Herod the Great and named after his early benefactor, Mark Antony (*J.W.* 5:238–245). Recent excavations, however, have determined that the *Lith-*

ostrotos (John 19:13)—the pavement where tradition remembers Pilate condemned Jesus—under the present-day Church of Ecce Homo, dates from the time of Hadrian (c. A.D. 135) and not from the New Testament period.

Instead, Pilate was probably staying in the palace of Herod the Great on the western hill. Both Philo (*Legat.* 38:299) and Josephus (*J.W.* 2:31) report that Herod's palace in Jerusalem was the residence of the Roman governor. According to Mark, Herod's palace was also called the Praetorium: "The soldiers led Jesus away into the palace, that is the Praetorium" (Mark 15:16a). Later, we read that the Roman governor resided in Herod's seaside palace in Caesarea that is similarly called the Praetorium of Herod (Acts 23:35).

Inscription mentioning "Pontius Pilatus," from the Roman theater at Caesarea. (NEAEHL)

Luke reports that Jesus was charged with stirring up the population from Galilee to Jerusalem, encouraging the people not to pay taxes and claiming to be the king Messiah (Luke 23:2). When his accusers informed Pilate that he came from Galilee, the prefect sought to pass Jesus off to Herod Antipas, tetrarch of Galilee and Perea. Antipas was staying in the former Hasmonean palace (*Ant.* 20:190). Its location has not been confirmed, but it may have been

Scale model of the Antonia Fortress, at the northwest corner of the Temple Mount, looking east. (photo S. Magal)

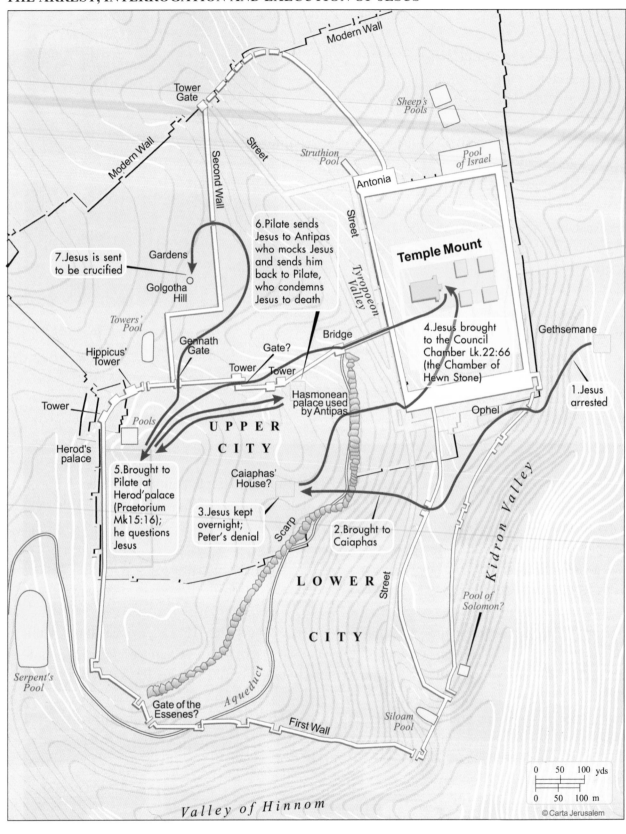

7. Jesus is sent to be crucified

6. Pilate sends Jesus to Antipas who mocks Jesus and sends him back to Pilate, who condemns Jesus to death

4. Jesus brought to the Council Chamber Lk.22:66 (the Chamber of Hewn Stone)

1. Jesus arrested

5. Brought to Pilate at Herod'palace (Praetorium Mk15:16); he questions Jesus

3. Jesus kept overnight; Peter's denial

2. Brought to Caiaphas

Caiaphas' House?

Hasmonean palace used by Antipas

Temple Mount

Gethsemane

Golgotha Hill

Gardens

Tower Gate

Modern Wall

Second Wall

Street

Struthion Pool

Antonia

Pool of Israel

Sheep's Pools

Hippicus' Tower

Gennath Gate

Tower

Gate?

Bridge

Tower

Towers' Pool

Tower

Pools

Herod's palace

U P P E R   C I T Y

L O W E R   C I T Y

Tyropoeon Valley

Street

Kidron Valley

Ophel

Pool of Solomon?

Scarp

Serpent's Pool

Gate of the Essenes?

Aqueduct

First Wall

Street

Siloam Pool

Valley of Hinnom

0 50 100 yds
0 50 100 m

© Carta Jerusalem

north of the neighborhood of the priestly homes previously mentioned. In any event, all of these sites were closely situated.

Josephus and the Gospels record that Antipas executed John the Baptist, the cousin of Jesus (*Ant.* 18:119; Matt 14:3–12; Mark 6:17–29). John had openly criticized the marriage of Antipas and his second wife, Herodias. According to Josephus, the Herodian couple had divorced their spouses to legitimize a pre-existing adulterous affair, an action prohibited according to Jewish law (*m. Sotah* 5:1; *Ant.* 18:109–110; Matt 14:4; Mark 6:18). The popularity of John's movement together with his open rebuke had resulted in his tragic murder. Jesus may have subsequently taken up his cousin's reprimand (Luke 16:18). Antipas had been seeking to meet Jesus face to face (Luke 13:31–33, 23:8), but at their encounter Jesus remained silent. It seems the tetrarch did not interpret Jesus as great a threat as his cousin, so he returned the Galilean to Pilate in mocking attire (Luke 23:11–12).

Tiberius Caesar, emperor at the time of Jesus' death. (photo R. S. Notley)

Returned to Herod's palace, Pilate attempted to punish Jesus and release him, but the priestly family who had been the subject of Jesus' public rebuke pressed for his execution. The Roman prefect had a reputation as remembered by Josephus and Philo for his brutality, "a man of inflexible, stubborn and cruel disposition," guilty of "venality, violence, robbery, assault, abusive behavior, frequent executions without trial, and endless savage ferocity" (Philo *Legat.* 301–302; cf. 303–305; *Ant.* 18:55–59, 60–62; *J.W.* 2:175–177).

There is an additional facet of Pilate's character. His small temple built in Caesarea in honor of Tiberius is the only known temple built by a Roman official for a living emperor. Pilate's efforts to ingratiate himself with the emperor—who according to Suetonius (Suet. *Tib.* 26) forbade temples dedicated to himself—reveals another aspect of the prefect's complex personality, a personal weakness at the point of persuasion put forward by Jesus' accusers. "If you release [Jesus], you are no friend of Caesar" (John 19:12). Pilate condemned Jesus to death by crucifixion, and he was summarily led a short distance outside of the city to be executed.

Since the medieval period the *Via Dolorosa* ("the way of suffering") has been traced through the streets of Jerusalem, beginning at the site of the Antonia, east of today's Church of the Holy Sepulcher. Yet, there are early Byzantine traditions that remember the place where Jesus was flogged on Mount Zion (Bordeaux Pilgrim 592). These Christian traditions have confusedly combined the event of Jesus' flogging with his brief confinement at the House of Caiaphas. Yet, the Gospels record that it was Pilate's soldiers who flogged Jesus while he was still in the Praetorium (Matt 27:26; Mark 15:15). With the recent recognition that the Roman prefect was at Herod's former palace on the western hill, the Byzantine tradition may be a vestige of a pre-Byzantine memory concerning the location of Jesus' Roman incarceration, flogging and condemnation to death.

If modern scholarship is correct, then the starting point for Jesus' way of suffering began on the western hill, today's Mount Zion. He was led from Herod's palace and out the city gates to be crucified. Excavations directed south of the Muristan in the Old City of Jerusalem discovered portions

The traditional site of Jesus' tomb, inside the rotunda of the Church of the Holy Sepulcher. (photo S. Magal)

of the First Wall of Jerusalem described by Josephus. More important for our present interests is the discovery of the remains of a first-century gate, thought to be the one mentioned by Josephus. He describes only one gate along the northern line of the First Wall, the Gennath Gate: "The second wall started from the gate in the first wall which they called Gennath (i.e., Garden Gate), and [the second wall] enclosing only the northern district of the town, went up as far as Antonia" (*J.W.* 5:146).

If Jesus was taken from Herod's palace to the area north of the walled city as Christian tradition remembers, then it seems likely that he would have been taken out of the city through the Gennath Gate. Josephus does not discuss the etymology of the name of the gate, but the Fourth Gospel may assist. It supplies a unique topographical detail on the vicinity where Jesus was executed, "in the place where [Jesus] was crucified there was a garden" (John 19:41). John's description of an agricultural area north of the city corresponds to the etymology of the Gennath Gate. The gate opened northward beyond the First Wall of Jerusalem to an area of gardens. It is in this area that Christian tradition marks the place of Jesus' death, burial and resurrection.

Twenty years of excavations as part of restoration work within the Church of the Holy Sepulcher have helped to determine the early history of the site. It was the location of a limestone quarry during the Old Testament period. Unfortunately, the traditional tomb of Jesus has been severely damaged over the centuries, and visitors can see little of the original hewn stone. Nevertheless, the so-called Tomb of Nicodemus and Joseph of Arimathea nearby is typical of a first-century *kokh* tomb.

The topographical question at the center of the claims of the Church of the Holy Sepulcher is whether the site was inside or outside the walls of first-century Jerusalem. Since no conclusive evidence has been discovered from Josephus' Second Wall (which would determine the position of the present-day church vis-à-vis the city walls in A.D. 30), the presence of Jewish tombs—which were required to be outside the boundary of a city—within the Church of the Holy Sepulcher may be the best evidence that the traditional site of Golgotha was indeed outside the walls of first-century Jerusalem. The site remains the best candidate for the place of Jesus' death, burial and resurrection.

CHAPTER 9

FROM THE EMPTY TOMB TO THE ROAD TO EMMAUS

THE GOSPELS are in agreement that Jesus died on a Friday afternoon as the Sabbath approached (Matt 27:45; Mark 15:33; Luke 23:44; John 19:31, 42). According to Luke 23:46, his dying words were uttered from Psalm 31:5 [HMT 31:6], the traditional deathbed prayer of an observant Jew: "Into your hand, I commit my spirit." Those who had accompanied Jesus were concerned that his corpse not remain exposed overnight. Josephus attests to a similar Jewish concern in the wake of Titus' crucifixion of countless innocent victims during the siege of Jerusalem.

> [The Romans] actually went so far in their impiety as to cast out the corpses without burial, although the Jews are so careful about funeral rites that even malefactors who have been sentenced to crucifixion are taken down and buried before sunset. (*J.W.* 4:317)

The initiative to provide Jesus with a proper burial (cf. *m. Naz.* 6:5; 7:1 [Lev 21:1]) was taken by Nicodemus and Joseph from Arimathea (Matt 27:57; Mark 15:43; Luke 23:20; John 19:38–42), leading figures in the city. Nicodemus is well known from rabbinic literature and was a wealthy patrician of Jerusalem (John 7:50–52; *b. Giṭ.* 56a; *t. 'Erub.* 3[4]:17). The provision of a burial place for one who could not afford his own would have been part of these aristocrats' expected role to dispense charity.

Although there was urgency to assure that Jesus was properly interred before sunset, there was insufficient time to prepare his body. "It was the day of Preparation [for the Sabbath, i.e., Friday], and the Sabbath was beginning" (Luke 23:54). The women who had accompanied Jesus from Galilee took the responsibility for the preparation. So, they followed and noted the location of the tomb, determined to return after the Sabbath to complete their task.

Of all the variants in the resurrection accounts, two geographical notes in those reports cannot be overlooked: Jesus' reported resurrection appearance in Galilee and the site identification of Emmaus.

Paul of Tarsus penned the oldest literary witness to the Christian belief in Jesus' resurrection from the dead.

> For I delivered to you as of first importance what I also received that Christ died for our sins in accordance with the scriptures, that he was buried, that he was raised on the third day in accordance with the scriptures, and that he appeared to Cephas, then to the twelve. Then he appeared to more than five hundred brethren at one time, most of whom are still alive, though some have fallen asleep. (1 Cor 15:3–6)

The Apostle mentions several resurrection appearances by Jesus, some of which are not repeated elsewhere in the New Testament. However, he also refers to an individual appearance to Cephas (i.e., Simon Peter; John 1:42; 1 Cor 1:12, 3:22, 9:5; Gal 1:18, 2:9) that is included in Luke's story of Jesus' encounter with the two departing Jerusalem on the road to Emmaus. When the two returned that evening to Jerusalem to tell those gathered what had happened, they were told, "The Lord has risen indeed, and has appeared to Simon!" (Luke 24:34).

The report of an individual appearance to Simon Peter, as distinguished from the other followers of Jesus, is not preserved in Mark and Matthew, but it may be the genesis for Mark's specific mention of Peter in the instruction to the women at the empty tomb, "But go, tell his disciples and Peter that he is going before you to Galilee; there you will see him, as he told you" (Mark 16:7; cf. Matt 28:7). The fragmented endings in the manuscripts of Mark's Gospel present a challenge for text critics. However, the various endings of Mark include neither an individual appearance to Peter nor any appearance of Jesus in Galilee.

The singling out of Peter in the Markan logion is likely to address the unreconciled breach between Jesus and Peter, which resulted from the disciple's denial of his master (Matt 26:69–75 *parr.*). Although the Fourth Gospel does not preserve Mark's logion and the anticipated encounter, reconciliation between Peter and Jesus is certainly central to the episode recorded in John 21:15–19. In other words, the Johannine account of Peter and Jesus on the shores of the Sea of Galilee is the literary complement to the unfulfilled expectations raised in the Markan statement at the empty tomb.

Notwithstanding the Evangelists' motives in their concern for Peter, it should be noted that there is no reason to read Paul's statement as a testimony of Jesus' appearance to Peter in Galilee. Indeed, what is striking about the Pauline version of Christianity's most primitive resurrection tradition is the absence of any knowledge of a Galilee appearance by Jesus. Paul seems unaware of the traditions preserved in Matthew 28:16 or John 21:15–19 that Jesus appeared to the eleven in Galilee. Moreover, if recent scholarship is correct, that John 20:30–31 served at an earlier stage of composition to conclude the Fourth Gospel, then John's earliest testimony without the epilogue of

The rolling stone in Herod's family tomb, Jerusalem. This was a common feature of the period.

Statue of the risen Christ before Peter, located outside the Church of the Primacy along the shore of the Sea of Galilee. (photo S. Magal)

THE RESURRECTION AND ASCENSION

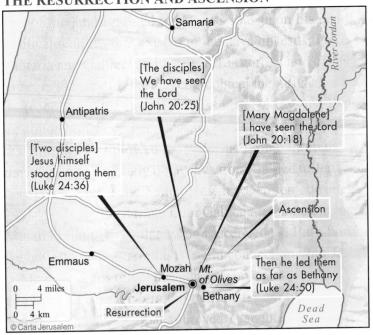

© Carta Jerusalem

chapter 21 agrees with Paul, Luke and the extant endings of Mark, all of which lack a report of Jesus' appearance to his followers in Galilee after the resurrection.

These witnesses concur with Luke's presentation—which is too often easily discarded by New Testament scholarship as the Evangelist's attempt to anticipate the literary structure of his sequel (cf. Acts 1:8)—that the followers of Jesus remained in Jerusalem until the outpouring of the Holy Spirit at Pentecost. According to the Third Gospel, Jesus instructed them, "And behold, I send the promise of my Father upon you; *but stay in the city*, until you are clothed with power from on high" (Luke 24:49).

As a brief aside, this type of expanded narrative witnessed in the post–Easter Galilee appearances of Matthew, John (and assumed in the logion of Mark), is seen elsewhere in the Synoptic tradition. The incidental mention of a term or toponym in one Gospel serves as the seed for a developed narrative tradition in a parallel account. This expansive style of storytelling shares affinities with contemporary Jewish Midrash, Targums and intertestamental literature that presents the Bible creatively rewritten (e.g., Jubilees, Genesis Apocryphon, etc.).

In the arrest of Jesus, Luke's singular mention of the Sanhedrin (Luke 22:66) to designate the council-chamber, in Mark and Matthew became the historical kernel for the illegal night-meeting of the full Sanhedrin (Matt 26:59; Mark 14:55) and their condemnation of Jesus. This is not to suggest literary dependence, but only access to common sources. Although not of great significance, it should come as no surprise that John's Gospel agrees with Luke in his omission of any participation of the Sanhedrin or a night-trial by the ruling council in Jerusalem.

In the current narrative, Luke preserves a statement by the two angelic men at the empty tomb.

Why do you seek the living among the dead? Remember how he told you, *while he was still in Galilee*, that the Son of man must be delivered into the hands of sinful men, and be crucified, and on the third day rise.

(Luke 24:5b–7)

Consider Mark's version of the same statement, "But go, tell his disciples and Peter that he is going before you to Galilee; there you will see him, as he told you" (Mark 16:7). While Matthew 28:7 agrees with Mark that the disciples are instructed to go to Galilee, he does not preserve the notion that Jesus himself informed them of this earlier, concluding instead, "Behold, I have told you." It seems that first-century reports circulated concerning the encounter at the empty tomb with mention of Galilee, and these provided the narrative seeds from which "the Galilee appearance" traditions emerged. Yet, the earliest testimony in the New Testament reported by Paul is silent on the Galilee appearances of the resurrected Jesus.

The Valley of Ayalon (biblical Aijalon). At center right a partial view is seen of 'Imwas, popularly identified with New Testament Emmaus.
(photo S. Ben-Yosef)

As we began, mention by Paul of an appearance to Simon Peter is echoed in the report given to the two who returned from Emmaus, already on the eve of the first day of the week. The identification of the destination for those two has been the subject of speculation. Christian tradition since the Byzantine period has uniformly identified New Testament Emmaus with Nicopolis-'Imwas. This identification, however, is not without its difficulties. Luke describes the location of Emmaus, "sixty stadia (seven miles) from Jerusalem." The traditional site of Nicopolis-'Imwas exceeds that distance, situated approximately 22 miles (35 km) from Jerusalem.

The discrepancy in distance between Luke's description and the Byzantine city is likely the cause for the textual changes in some manuscripts to read "one hundred and sixty stadia" in Luke 24:13. The revised distance brought the location of New Testament Emmaus in line with the

Remains of the Roman road leading from Jerusalem to Emmaus. (photo R. S. Notley)

Byzantine identification of the site with Nicopolis-'Imwas. So, according to Eusebius' *Onomasticon*, "Emmaus: From whence came Cleopas, who is recorded in the Gospel according to Luke. This is now Nicopolis, the famous *polis* of Palaestina" (Eus. *Onom.* 90:15). However, the editorial committee of the United Bible Society's Greek New Testament determined that in spite of the difficulties in site identification, the best reading is the shorter distance of "sixty stadia" attested in better manuscripts. Our identification of New Testament Emmaus must fall within the spatial limits imposed by the best manuscript readings, thus excluding Nicopolis-'Imwas.

It seems that early Christian tradition exchanged the identity of a lesser known village by the same name for the Byzantine metropolis. Josephus knew both locations. The site of Emmaus at Nicopolis-'Imwas is given as the location for the encampment of attacking foreign forces during the Hasmonean Revolt (*Ant.* 12:298, 306; 13:15) and the First Jewish Revolt (*J.W.* 5:42). However, Josephus knew another Emmaus closer to Jerusalem. After the Jewish Revolt Vespasian assigned "eight hundred veterans discharged from the army a place for habitation called Emmaus, distant thirty stadia (3.5 miles) from Jerusalem" (*J.W.* 7:217; cf. *m. Suk.* 4:5; *y. Suk.* 54b; *b. Suk.* 45a). The distance is precisely half of the distance (i.e., sixty stadia) described in Luke's Gospel, perhaps suggesting that Luke's measurement includes the return distance to Jerusalem. In any event, the description that the two returned that very evening to Jerusalem indicates that the village of Emmaus was nearby to Jerusalem and more likely the place mentioned by Josephus.

INDEX

A

Abba Saul b. Batnit   69, 70
Abel-beth-maacah   29
Abila; Abila Lysanias   28, 52, 56
Abil el-Qamh   29
Abraham   54
Acre. *See* Ptolemais
Aenon   14, 16, 17
Agrippa I   41, 45
Agrippa II   34, 41, 45
Agrippina   20
Aijalon/Ayalon Valley   81
Akiva, Rabbi   71
Alexander (clan of Annas)   71
Alexander Jannaeus. *See* Jannaeus, Alexander
Alexandria   13
Amman   6. *See also* Philadelphia
Ammathus   20
Andrew   18, 33, 36, 39, 46
Annas   60, 70, 71
Antipas   18, 25, 31, 32, 33, 41, 45, 73, 74, 75. *See also* Herod Antipas
Antipatris   56, 80
Antonia Fortress (Jerusalem)   68, 72, 73, 74, 75, 76
Apollonia   56
Arabah   6
Araj, el-   39. *See also* Khirbet el-Araj
Arav, Rami   42
Arbela   20
Arbel Pass   23
Archelais   10
Archelaus   10, 11, 13, 45, 56
Arculf   36
Aristobulus I   26
Arnon River   6, 52
Ascalon   10, 13
Ascent of Adummim   56
Asochis   20

A (continued)

Augustus Caesar   9, 41, 53
Auranitis   10
Aviam, Mordechai   39
Avi-Yonah, Michael   42
Azotus   10

B

Banias   6, 29. *See also* Caesarea Philippi
Baptist, The   32. *See also* John (the Baptist)
Bar'am   38
Bar Kathros   69, 70
Bar Kokhba rebellion   37
Bartameus   56
Bashan   6, 14, 17, 18, 19, 43. *See also* Batanea
Batanea   10, 14, 18, 19
Beautiful Gate   68
Beersheba   6
Beit Safafa   62
Bersabe   20
Besara   20
Bethabara   14, 16, 17
Bethany (beyond the Jordan)   16, 17, 18
Bethany (nr. Jerusalem)   6, 56, 57, 58, 65, 69, 80
Bethany (region)   14. *See also* Bashan; Batanea
Beth-haccerem Valley   21
Beth-horon Ridge   56
Bethlehem   6, 8, 9, 10
Bethmaus   20
Bethphage   56, 57
Bethsaida   6, 15, 19, 20, 28, 33, 35, 36, 37, 38, 39, 40, 41, 42, 43, 45, 46, 47, 53. *Also* Bethsaida-Julias
Beth-shean   45, 49, 50. *See also* Scythopolis
Bethso   62, 64
Bêt Netôfa Valley   21, 22, 23
Bliss, F. J.   62
Boethus   70
Burj el-Alawiyeh   29

C

Cadasa   20, 28

Caesarea   6, 10, 12, 13, 20, 28, 29, 30, 45, 56, 72, 73, 75. *Also* Caesarea Maritima   46

Caesarea Philippi   6, 10, 28, 29, 30, 51. *See also* Banias; Paneas

Caiaphas   69, 70, 71, 74, 75

—, House of   68

Cana   6, 14, 20, 21, 22, 23, 28

Canatha   52

Capercotnei   20

Capernaum   6, 14, 20, 21, 22, 23, 28, 29, 31, 33, 34, 35, 36, 37, 38, 43, 47, 56

Capitolias   52

Cenaculum (Jerusalem)   66

Cephas   78. *See also* Simon Peter

Chabulon   20

Chamber of Hewn Stone (Jerusalem)   58, 70, 71

Chorazin   6, 20, 33, 37, 38, 39, 43, 46

Christ. *See* Jesus

Chrysorrhoe river   51

Coastal Plain   6

Constantine   36

Council Chamber (Jerusalem)   74

D

Damascus   6, 29, 51, 52, 53

Damascus Gate (Jerusalem)   62

Dan   29. *See also* Caesarea Philippi; Paneas

Daphne   20

David   9, 69

Dead Sea   6, 10, 14, 52, 61, 64

Decapolis   28, 29, 51, 52, 53, 54

Diocaesarea   37. *See also* Sepphoris

Dion   28, 52

Dor   10, 20, 56

E

Ecdippa   20, 28

Edom   6

Edrei   52

Egeria   17, 35, 36, 37

Egypt   9, 11, 12, 13, 29

Ein Kerem   6

Ekron. *See* Tel Miqne

Eleazar ben Azariah   70

Elijah   15

El-Odeitha   29

Emmatha   20, 33

Emmaus   6, 56, 77, 78, 80, 81, 82

Ennion of Sidon   70

Epiphanius   36, 37

Er-Riha   57

Esbus   10, 13

Esdraelon (city)   20

Esdraelon Valley   6, 20

Essenes   61, 63, 64, 65, 66, 74

Essenes, Gate of the (Jerusalem)   62, 63, 64, 74

Eusebius   16, 17, 18, 22, 37, 38, 39, 43, 49, 50, 51, 52, 82

Exaloth   20

F

First Wall (Jerusalem)   62, 76

Flusser, David   26

G

Gabara   20, 21

Gadara   6, 10, 14, 20, 28, 33, 46, 47, 48, 49, 50, 51, 52, 53, 54, 56

Gadora (Gedor)   52

Galasa   52. *See also* Gerasa

Galilee   6, 9, 10, 13, 14, 18, 20, 21, 22, 23, 26, 27, 28, 29, 30, 31, 32, 33, 34, 37, 38, 39, 41, 46, 47, 48, 51, 52, 53, 56, 65, 73, 77, 78, 80

Galilee of the Gentiles   28

Gamala   6

Garis   20

Gate of the Essenes. *See* Essenes, Gate of the

Gath-hepher   20

Gaulanitis   10, 42, 48, 49

Gaza   6, 10, 13

Geba   10, 20, 28

Gedor   10. *See also* Gadora

Gelil-ha-goiim   28, 29. *See also* Galilee of the Gentiles

Gennath Gate (Jerusalem)   62, 74, 76

Gennesaret   20, 33, 47, 56

Gennesar/Gennesaret, Lake of   25, 26, 27, 29, 30, 33, 35, 40. *See also* Sea of Galilee

Gennesaret/Gennesar, Plain of   23, 26, 33, 35

Gerasa   6, 10, 13, 46, 47, 49, 50, 51. *See also* Jerash

Gergesa   20, 28, 33, 46, 49, 50, 51

Gergeshta. *See* Girgash

Geshur   44, 49

Gethsemane   25, 30, 68, 69, 74

Gilead   6

Ginae   56

Girgash   49, 50

Gischala   20, 28

Golan   6, 18, 43. *See also* Gaulanitis

Golgotha   25, 30, 68, 74, 76

Golgotha Hill   74

H

Haceldama   68

Hadrian   73

Haifa   6

Hammath Gader   37, 48, 54

Hammath(-Tiberias)   32

Hanin   59, 67, 70. *See also* Annas

Hannathon Valley   21

Harosheth-ha-goiim   28

Hasmoneans   26

Hauran   45, 51

Hebron   6

Heliopolis   32, 52

Heptapegon. *See* Tabgha

Hermon, Mount   18

Herod Antipas   10, 13, 18, 25, 28, 31, 56, 73

Herodias   75

Herodion; Herodium   6, 11

Herod I (the Great)   9, 10, 11, 13, 45, 46, 53, 56, 57, 72, 73, 74, 75

Herod Philip   10, 40, 41, 45, 56

Herod's Family Tomb(s)   68, 78

Heshbon   13

Hina   52

Hinnom Valley   74

Hippicus Tower (Jerusalem)   62, 64, 74

Hippus   6, 10, 20, 28, 33, 48, 52, 53, 56

Holy Sepulcher, Church of the   75, 76

Holy Zion, Basilica of   68

Honorius, Julius   25

Hula Valley   6

Hyrcanus, John   26, 27

I

Idumea   10

Iraq al-Amir   6

Isaiah   13, 15, 16, 28, 29, 30, 51

Ishmael (the son of Phabi)   70

Issi, Rabbi   37

Iturea   52

J

Jaffa Gate (Jerusalem)   62

Jamnia   10

Jamnith   20

Jannaeus, Alexander   26, 27

Janoah   28

Japhia   20

Jaubert, Annie   61

Jerash   47. *See also* Gerasa

Jericho   6, 13, 14, 18, 56, 57

Jerome   52

Jerusalem   6, 9, 10, 11, 13, 14, 15, 16, 26, 31, 46, 52, 55, 56, 57, 58, 61, 62, 63, 64, 65, 67, 68, 69, 70, 71, 72, 73, 75, 76, 77, 78, 80, 81, 82

Jesus   9, 11, 13, 14, 15, 16, 17, 18, 19, 20, 21, 22, 23, 25, 28, 29, 30, 31, 33, 34, 37, 39, 40, 41, 46, 47, 49, 51, 54, 55, 56, 57, 58, 59, 60, 61, 64, 65, 66, 67, 68, 69, 70, 71, 72, 73, 74, 75, 76, 77, 78, 80

Jewish Revolt (against Rome)   34, 41, 42, 52, 53, 82

Jezreel Valley   21, 28

John (clan of Annas)   71

John Hyrcanus. *See* Hyrcanus, John

John (the Baptist)   9, 13, 14, 15, 16, 17, 18, 19, 61, 75

John (the Evangelist)   9, 16, 22, 27, 76, 78, 80

Jonathan (Maccabeus)   26

Joppa   10, 13, 56

Jordan River   6, 10, 14, 16, 17, 18, 20, 28, 37, 40, 41, 42, 43, 48, 52, 55, 56, 80

Jordan Valley   6, 15, 18, 21

Joseph bar Caiapha   69. *See also* Caiaphas

Joseph (husband of Mary)   9, 11, 13

Joseph (of Arimathea)   76, 77

—, Tomb of   68

Joseph (of Tiberias)   36

Josephus   9, 10, 18, 21, 22, 23, 25, 26, 27, 31, 32, 34, 39, 40, 41, 43, 45, 48, 51, 62, 63, 64, 66, 67, 73, 75, 76, 77, 82

Jotapata   20, 22, 28, 41

Judas Iscariot   69

Judea/Judaea   6, 10, 11, 14, 15, 52, 56, 72

Judean Desert   6. *See also* Wilderness of Judea

Judgment Gate (Jerusalem)   68

Julias   10, 40, 41, 43, 45. *See also* Bethsaida

Justus   48

K

Kafr Aqib   43

Kafr Kana   22

Kanah   22

Kathros   70

Kefar Akabia   33

Kefar-dan   20

Khirbet el-Araj   43. *See also* Araj, el-

Khirbet el-Mafjar   57

Khirbet Karazzeh   38

Khirbet Qanah   22, 23. *See also* Cana

Khirbet Qumran   66. *See also* Qumran

Kidron Valley   74

Kinneret, Sea of   27. *See also* Sea of Galilee

Kishon River   28

Kohl, H.   37, 38

Kuhn, Heinz-Wolfgang   42

Kursi   33, 44, 47, 50, 51. *See also* Gergesa

L

Ladder of Tyre   20, 28

Lake Tiberias. *See* Sea of Galilee

Lazarus   58

Litani River   6

Livias   10

Livia (wife of Augustus)   41

Lower Galilee   20

Luke   9, 13, 16, 27, 30, 47, 51, 55, 56, 58, 59, 60, 65, 69, 70, 73, 77, 78, 80, 81, 82

Lydda   56

M

Machaerus/Macherus   6, 18

Magdala   6, 20, 23, 33, 34. *See also* Taricheae

Magness, Jodi   66

Maritime Gadara   33

Maritime Hippus   33

Mark   9, 15, 16, 18, 19, 27, 29, 30, 40, 47, 51, 53, 58, 60, 69, 73, 78, 80

Martha (sister of Lazarus)   56, 58

Mary Magdalene   33, 80

Mary (mother of Jesus)   9, 13

Mary (sister of Lazarus)   56, 58

Masada   6

Matthew   9, 10, 11, 12, 13, 15, 16, 21, 27, 28, 29, 30, 33, 47, 51, 53, 58, 60, 69, 78, 80

Mediterranean Sea   6, 10, 13, 20, 29, 52

Memphis   13

Meron   20

Mesadiyeh   43

Mezad Hasidim   14

Moab   6

Moses   19

Mount Carmel   6, 10, 20

Mount Ephraim   56

Mount Gilboa   6

Mount Hermon   6

Mount Nebo   6

Mount of Olives   50, 57, 60, 68, 69, 80

Mount of Temptation   6

Mount Tabor   6, 14, 20, 56

Mount Zion   61, 63, 64, 65, 66, 67, 75

Mozah   80

N

Nabateans   10, 13

Nablus   6. *See also* Shechem

Nahal 'Amud   26

Nain   20

Naphtali   28

Nathana-el   22

Nazareth   6, 9, 11, 12, 13, 14, 20, 21, 22, 23, 28, 31, 34, 37, 56

Negev   6
Nero   34
Nicodemus   76, 77
Nicopolis-'Imwas   81, 82
Nile River   13
Nun, Mendel   39
Nysa   51, 52. *See also* Scythopolis

O

Ophel   74
Origen   16, 17, 49, 50, 51

P

Palatial Mansion (Jerusalem)   70, 71
Palestine   52
Paneas   10, 29. *See also* Caesarea Philippi; Paneas
Passover   55, 58, 60, 61, 64, 65, 66, 67, 69, 72
Paul   65, 67, 77, 78, 80, 81
Pausanias   25
Pella   6, 10, 52
Pelusium   13
Perea/Peraea   6, 10, 13, 14, 47, 52, 55, 56, 73
Peter   18, 33, 34, 36, 39, 46, 74, 78, 79, 80. *See also* Simon Peter
Peter the Deacon   35
Petra   13
Pharisees   10
Phasaelis   10
Pheroras   10
Philadelphia   6, 10, 13. *See also* Amman
Philadelphia (Rabbath-ammon)   51, 52. *See also* Amman
Philip (son of Herod)   40, 41, 45, 46. *See also* Herod Philip
Philip (the Evangelist)   18, 33, 39, 46
Philistines   54
Philo   73, 75
Philoteria   33, 52
Phoenicia   10, 51
Pilate   75. *See also* Pontius Pilate
Pliny (the Elder)   26, 34, 41, 42, 51, 52
Pompey   53
Pontius Pilate   55, 72, 73, 74
Pool of Israel (Jerusalem)   68, 74

Pool of Solomon (Jerusalem)   74
Potter's Field. *See* Haceldama
Praetorium (Jerusalem)   68, 72, 73, 75
Ptolemais   6, 10, 13, 20, 21, 22, 23, 28, 37, 52, 56. *See also* Acre
Ptolemy   41, 42, 52

Q

Qalat Marun   29
Qarné Hittim   23
Qasr el-Yahud   19
Quaresmius   22
Quirinius   9
Qumran   6, 14, 62, 63, 64, 67
Qumran Congregation   15, 61, 63, 64, 66

R

Rabb Thelathin   29
Rainey, Anson F.   28, 29
Raphana   51, 52
Robinson, Edward   39
Romans   55, 70, 77
Rome   11, 34, 46, 53

S

Saab   20
Saana   52
Sahl el-Battôf. *See* Bêt Netôfa Valley
Salim   14, 16, 17
Samaria (city)   13, 46, 80. *See also* Sebaste
Samaria (region)   6, 10, 11, 14, 17, 48, 52, 56
Samaritans   56
Samulis   52
Sanhedrin   70, 71, 80
Sapsaphas   17
Schumacher, Gottlieb   39
Scythopolis   6, 10, 14, 17, 20, 48, 49, 50, 51, 52, 53, 55, 56. *See also* Beth-shean; Nysa
Sea of Galilee   6, 14, 18, 19, 20, 21, 22, 23, 24, 25, 26, 27, 28, 29, 30, 31, 33, 34, 37, 39, 40, 42, 43, 47, 48, 49, 50, 51, 56, 78, 79
Sebaste   6, 10, 14, 45, 56. *See also* Samaria (city)
Second Wall (Jerusalem)   76
Sennabris   20, 33

Sepph   20

Sepphoris   6, 10, 14, 20, 21, 23, 28, 37, 44, 45, 56

Serpent's Pool (Jerusalem)   74

Shaghûr, esh-   21

Shalem, Dina   39

Sharon   6

Shechem   6. *See also* Nablus

Sheep's Pools (Jerusalem)   68, 74

Shephelah   6

Sidon (city)   6, 28, 29, 51

Sidon (district)   28

Siloam Pool (Jerusalem)   68, 74

Siloam Tower (Jerusalem)   68

Simon Bar-Jona   28

Simonias   20, 21

Simon (Maccabeus)   26

Simon Peter   78, 81. *See* Cephas; *See also* Peter

Sogane   20

Solinus   25, 26

Solomon's Portico (Jerusalem)   68

Strabo   26, 52

Struthion Pool   74

Suetonius   75

Susa   62

Sycaminum   20

Syria   9, 10, 46, 51, 52, 56

Syro-Phoenicia   52

T

Tabgha (Heptapegon)   6, 33, 35

Tarfon, Rabbi   71

Taricheae   20, 21, 22, 23, 26, 28, 32, 34. *See also* Magdala

Tel Aviv-Jaffa   6

Tell el-Hassan   57

Tell, et-   39, 41, 42, 43, 44, 45, 46

Tell el-Qâdī   29, 40. *See also* Dan

Tell es-Sultan   57

Tell Samara   48

Tel Miqne (Ekron)   40

Temple (Jerusalem)   68, 74

Temple Mount   58, 59, 60, 63, 68, 73, 74

Thella   20

Tiberias   6, 10, 10–88, 14, 18, 20, 21, 23, 25, 26, 28, 31, 32, 33, 34, 36, 37, 44, 45, 48, 56

Tiberius   41, 75

Titus   77

Tomb of the Virgin (Jerusalem)   68

Tower Gate (Jerusalem)   74

Towers' Pool (Jerusalem)   68, 74

Trachonitis   10

Transjordan   56

Turân Basin/Valley   21

Tyre (city)   6, 10, 20, 28, 29, 51

Tyre (district)   28, 51

Tyropoeon Valley   68, 74

U

Umm Qeis   6, 47. *See also* Gadara; Hammath Gader

V

Van de Velde, C. W. M.   38

Vespasian   51, 52, 82

Via Dolorosa   68, 75

W

Wadi Qelt   57

Wâdī Samekh   49

Watzinger, C.   37, 38

Way to (of) the Sea   28, 29, 51

Wilderness of Judea   14, 16, 17

Willibald   36

X

Xenereth (or Xenera), Sea of   27. *See also* Sea of Galilee

Y

Yanuh   29

Yarmuk River   18, 51

Z

Zacchaeus   56

Zebulun   28